PIPPA GREENWOOD'S GARDENING YEAR

PIPPA GREENWOOD'S GARDENING YEAR

headline

First published in 2004
by HEADLINE BOOK PUBLISHING

10 9 8 7 6 5 4 3 2 1

Cataloguing in Publication Data is available from the British Library

ISBN 0 7553 1083 7

Set in Rotis and Helvetica by Ben Cracknell Studios
Designed by Ben Cracknell Studios
Edited by Anne Askwith
Special photography by Sarah Heneghan
Picture Research Mel Watson

Colour reproduction by Spectrum Colour, Ipswich

Printed and bound in Italy by Canale S.p.A

Headline's policy is to use papers that are natural, renewable and recyclable
products and made from wood grown in sustainable forests. The logging and
manufacturing processes are expected to conform to the environmental
regulations of the country of origin.

HEADLINE BOOK PUBLISHING
A division of Hodder Headline
338 Euston Road
London NW1 3BH

www.headline.co.uk
www.hodderheadline.com

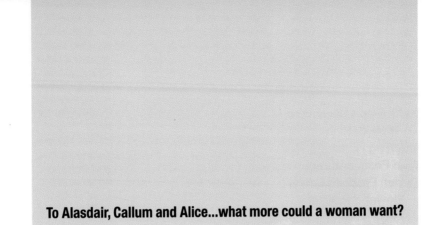

To Alasdair, Callum and Alice...what more could a woman want?

CONTENTS

INTRODUCTION

WE ALL KNOW the problem: a garden sitting outside the back door, and possibly one out the front too, a strong desire to have these potentially great spaces looking good, and not enough time to do everything that you think you ought to be doing. I am a great believer that a garden should be a pleasure to have, maintain and develop, and not a millstone that constantly weighs on your conscience. But it can be difficult to know what to do when, and in what order: which tasks are more important than others and, if you suddenly find yourself with an hour or two free, which job to get on with first. This is the book for those who, all too often, find themselves in that position: a working person or a parent with a young family, or indeed anyone who has a host of other things taking up their potential gardening time – a situation I know and understand, because time is always my limiting factor.

The book is set out in month-by-month chapters so that when you find yourself with an hour or more to spare you can go to the appropriate month and see that, yes, now is the time to cut a hedge, plant up a border or whatever. Throughout, the emphasis is on jobs that, either in the short term or the long term, help to keep the time you spend on them to a minimum without compromising the end result and how your garden looks. In each month there are also suggestions for things to do which may seem like a bit of a slog but will save you time in the long term – applying a mulch, for instance, which will not only keep your plants happier but also reduce the time you will need to spend watering and weeding.

This is not the sort of gardening yearbook that tells you about absolutely everything. I have reduced the possibilities down to the sorts of things that I think you are likely to want to do and those that a busy person might actually be able to get around to doing. I am a keen fruit and vegetable grower, but I realise that this side of gardening is perhaps disproportionately time-consuming, and so the emphasis of the book is on those parts of the garden which those with smaller gardens and time-short gardeners are likely to concentrate on, the ornamentals, with some space devoted to edibles in case you have the room or time to grow them.

Each month is divided into sections relating to the main components of the garden – trees, shrubs and climbers, flowers (including containers), lawns, herbs and vegetables, fruit, and water features and ponds – and to non-plant elements such as fences, sheds and furniture. So, if in any month you know that one area of your garden is in need of attention, you can simply turn straight to the appropriate section to find out what you should be doing.

At the end of each section I have narrowed down the suggested jobs further into lists of 'Essentials' – jobs that have been explained in the section to which you should give priority if time is extremely short. Yes, the term 'prioritise' may not be something you associate with gardening, but that is just what I have done. There are, of course, plenty of things that need doing in the garden several times a year, or may be done in any of several months, and so there is a good amount of cross-referencing from one month to another.

My hope is that this book will enable you to feel happier with your garden, and to feel that you are working side by side with it, never at loggerheads with it, and enjoying it throughout the seasons.

January

It may seem as if the world consists purely of ice, frost, cold, dark and perhaps even a good helping of damp, but don't let the gloomier aspects of January get you down. Surely there is nothing much more beautiful than a really bright, sunny albeit icy cold day? True, the weather may mean that there are quite a number of tasks you can't easily get on with in the garden or, indeed, that there are a good few things you would be better off delaying, but there is still a plentiful supply of things you can do if you have the time.

For me January is often a month when I plan and try to think ahead to gardening aspirations for the rest of the year and also try to crack on with some of the less plant-orientated jobs – some tidying up or maybe even a bit of construction, who knows, but there is nothing better than a bit of gardening on a bright January day to clear away the cobwebs and cheer you up.

GENERAL TASKS

THE CHANCES ARE that the worst of the cold weather is still to come, so get on and ensure that everything that could possibly need winter protection is adequately snug and cared for. It is important not to be fooled by the fact that some plants have remained untouched by the weather so far, as January and February can be a lot crueller than the earlier parts of winter.

Check insulation around outside taps and lag pipework if necessary (see page 148).

Collect up any fallen leaves and twigs that have landed anywhere in the garden and add them to the compost heap or leaf mould pile. Any sizeable twigs may need to be shredded or at least broken up into small pieces first.

A double layer of bubble wrap will keep off all but the harshest weather, so reducing the risk of pipework becoming frozen

Tree ties may need adjusting from time to time; always allow a little room for expansion and keep the buffer in position between trunk and stake

TREES, SHRUBS AND CLIMBERS

ESSENTIALS

If time is really short, try to fit these jobs in.

- Provide or add to winter protection for plants that need it, and don't forget the garden tap.
- Winter-prune wisterias.
- If the weather is dry and/or windy, water evergreens growing in containers.
- Plant bare-root trees, shrubs or hedging plants, and container-grown plants, if the weather is suitable.

MAKE SURE THAT any winter protection over less hardy or more recently planted shrubs, climbers or trees is still firmly in place.

Check tree stakes and tree ties regularly, as winter winds and excessively moist soil can cause stakes to move and ties to become displaced, and replace or reposition as necessary. Erect a wind-break around relatively newly planted trees and shrubs in exposed areas to decrease the likelihood of them suffering winter damage or wind scorch. Make sure that the protection you provide allows plenty of air circulation, or else you may end up doing more harm than good.

Move any trees or shrubs that are in an unsuitable position, provided the soil is neither excessively wet nor frozen solid. Obviously it is better to do this when the plants are small, but if it is a case of either attempting to transplant it or getting rid of it completely, surely it is worth taking the risk? Increase your chances of success by ensuring you take as large a root ball as possible and then provide plenty of good aftercare.

Shorten the new shoots on wisteria to back to two or three buds from the main stem, using sharp secateurs. It is easier and quicker to do this pruning at this time of year, because you can readily see all the side shoots as they are not masked by leaves, and the great thing is that by doing it you will encourage plenty of flowering later in the year.

Restrict the growth of climbing hydrangeas, Boston ivy and Virginia creepers growing on walls or other vertical surfaces by trimming them back as necessary. Make sure that any ladders you use are safely supported.

Don't forget to water plants in containers. Anything that is producing even the slightest bit of growth will be using up a surprising amount of water and even if growth appear to be static, do not let the compost dry out completely. Evergreens, including conifers, are particularly likely to need a drink if the weather has been dry. They are prone to winter drought because they still have their leaves in place and so will still be losing a fair amount of moisture through transpiration, especially during windy conditions.

The roots must be well spread and the tree at the correct depth – a cane across the hole makes this easier to judge

out at all and so either heel in (temporarily plant) the plants in a more suitable part of the garden or wrap all the root systems in damp sacking and place the plants in a cool but frost-free position and ensure the roots never dry out. When conditions are more suitable you can then plant them. Whatever precautions you take, however, you must plant as soon as possible after you have brought the plants home or they have been delivered. Provided soil conditions are suitable you can also create hedges from container-grown hedging plants. For planting, see page 36.

Sow and plant

• Bare-root trees or shrubs are often available at this time of year and can be planted with great success now (see page 141). Young bare-root hedging plants also establish well if planted now (see page 151). However, if the soil is frozen solid or waterlogged when bare-root plants are delivered, it is best to delay planting. In the meantime it is essential to ensure that the root balls do not dry

FLOWERS

Draping a few layers of horticultural fleece over frost-prone blooms or plants should protect from a few degrees of frost

CHECK THAT THE CROWNS of herbaceous perennials and alpines are free from masses of damp claggy leaves from trees or shrubs near by. If left in place these can cause the crowns to deteriorate and they will also harbour pests such as snails and slugs.

Divide established or overgrown clumps of herbaceous perennials. Provided the soil is neither excessively wet nor frozen solid, you can safely divide most herbaceous perennials now (see page 119).

Early in the month, place a new mulch around the base of hellebores that flower at this time of year. A mulch of a fairly 'clean' material should help to minimise the amount of soil splash on to the flowers and the plants will of course benefit from the effects of the mulch.

If you want to try sowing a few summer-flowering bedding plants yourself this year, remember that many of these need to be sown in January if you are to benefit for the full length of the flowering season. Snapdragons, gazanias, pelargoniums and lobelias should all be sown now.

Top bulbs for summer-flowering

Lilies
Star of Bethlehem (Ornithogalum)
Wood hyacinths (*Galtonia candicans*)
Tigridia pavona
Alliums
Crinum

Regularly remove faded or weather-damaged flowers from winter bedding plants in borders or in containers. In damp weather these are especially prone to develop grey mould infections (see page 19), but these can largely be prevented if you keep up with the deadheading.

Regularly inspect any winter protection already in place on perennials and plants in containers and replace or refix as necessary.

Wrap the outer surface of containers with bubble wrap polythene, hessian or any other good insulating material, if you did not do so earlier in the winter. Plants growing in containers are far more susceptible to winter damage; root balls may become frozen and in extreme cases plants can be killed. Wrapping them up makes up for the fact that they are in exposed above-ground positions. Make sure that you leave the surface of the container and the drainage holes clear. You could place containers that can be safely moved in a more sheltered position, perhaps close to a house wall or an unheated greenhouse.

If the soil is not very wet, dig in bulky organic matter such as garden compost or well-rotted manure, to improve the texture and fertility of the soil. Doing this now may also disturb some weed seeds, stimulating them to germinate and so, in a few weeks' time, giving you the chance to hoe these off before you get planting – a great way of at least slightly reducing the number of weed problems you get once your plants are in the ground.

Sow and plant

• Think ahead to the summer and plant a good-sized pot with some lilies. Most lilies perform brilliantly in containers and look absolutely stunning, often providing colour, form and wonderful perfume. Good drainage is essential for these, so be sure to put plenty of crocks in the bottom of the container and use a free-draining compost, perhaps adding some extra grit. Or plant into a sunny, well-drained spot in the garden. On a heavy or wet soil, incorporate grit before planting and then dig a slightly deeper planting hole, filling the bottom 1–2cm ($\frac{1}{2}$–$\frac{3}{4}$in) with grit. Planting the bulb on its side helps to ensure a good display, as moisture is much less likely to get trapped in the scales of the bulb when it is planted in this way.

• Make good use of long, dark evenings or even a very wet miserable day and continue to choose seeds that you would like to order. Alternatively pay a visit to your favourite local garden centre and stock up on packets of seeds – it's got to be one of the cheapest forms of retail therapy I know!

• Sow yourself some sweet peas. All you need is a flowerpot or two, some multi-purpose compost and seeds of these delightful, delicate and heavenly scented plants. Cover the seeds with compost and keep them just moist. If you have a propagator a little bit of extra heat will bring them on faster, but provided the compost is kept moist and the surface does not dry out completely, you should be able to germinate the seeds well on a windowsill. When the seedlings are about 5–8cm (2–3in) tall, pinch out the tops.

• Treat yourself to a really gorgeous display of flowers this summer by ordering some summer-flowering bulbs. There should be a fair range of these in your local garden centre, or for an even better selection take a look at some of the specialist bulb catalogues. If you have always thought of bulbs as flowers that give a spring performance, it is time to think again. These can be planted between now and March.

THE LAWN

- Avoid walking on the lawn.

BRUSH OVER ANY PART of the lawn surface that has become covered with worm casts, using a besom or broom. Although the earthworms that produce these are obviously of huge benefit to the garden, a vital part of soil and garden health, the presence of casts on a lawn can be infuriating and cause problems if you are very lawn proud: the fine soil makes a perfect seedbed for weeds and if smeared over the surface of the lawn can cause slipperiness. If you brush the worm casts on a dry day, it will be easy to distribute the fine soil evenly but thinly over the lawn surface, rather like a top-dressing mixture.

Whenever possible, avoid walking on or working from the lawn when it is frosted or the ground is frozen – you can do an incredible amount of damage in a very short space of time and may also encourage infections such as snow mould. If you do need to walk across the lawn, try to wait until the surface has thawed or the frost has cleared. If you will be working for any length of time still cover the surface with planks or boards to distribute your weight more evenly.

If the surface of the lawn is not frozen, it may be worth carrying out a bit of temporary aeration using a garden fork (see page 125). Do not attempt this if the ground is very wet or else you may actually worsen the problem.

This is a perfect point in the year to check that your lawnmower is working properly, when your lawn is not taking up much effort or time. Take the mower to a service agent or set about the job yourself.

HERBS AND VEGETABLES

ESSENTIALS

If time is really short, try to fit these jobs in.

- Dig over the soil, add organic matter.
- Sow a few seeds of crops such as tomatoes for growing in a greenhouse.
- Buy or order vegetable seeds and seed potatoes.
- Chit seed potatoes as soon as they are delivered or you get them home.

Sow and plant

- Wear off a bit of excess energy by digging over any areas in which you intend to grow vegetables later on in the year. Incorporate plenty of bulky organic matter, such as garden compost or well-rotted manure. This will help to improve the soil texture and fertility and make watering less of a problem later in the year.

- If you have a greenhouse, it may be worth sowing a few seeds of edible plants so that you get some really early crops. However, if you live in one of the colder regions of the country, it would be best to wait until next month before doing this. Make sowings of greenhouse tomatoes and a few peppers and aubergines towards the end of the month. Sow a pot or two of basil indoors. If you are going to grow any of these crops outside you must not sow the seed yet.

- At the end of the month, make sowings of lettuce, cauliflowers and radish indoors. I prefer using cells to sowing in pots or trays because each plant has its own cube of compost and so can later be planted out with a well-developed and undisturbed root ball.

- Make sure that you have ordered or bought all the vegetable seeds you need. If you have not already done so, it is time to get your skates on and select precisely what you want to grow during the year ahead.

- Place orders for seed potatoes no later than this month; alternatively go down to your favourite local garden centre and see what they have available. Generally a much wider range can be purchased from seed or specialist catalogues. If possible, find out a bit about the varieties available by consulting a specialist book or catalogue – that way you can ensure that you get the taste and texture you really want. If you do not have much room to spare, but fancy growing potatoes, earlies or first earlies are usually your best option as they take up less space than maincrop potatoes, are in the ground for a shorter period of time, and will also produce a crop at a time of year when prices are particularly high.

- As soon as you have got hold of some seed tubers of early potatoes, you should chit them. All this means is that you need to place the potatoes with their blunt end uppermost in a tray and place the tray in a cool but frost-free, well-lit position. This will encourage the tiny 'eyes' on the potatoes' surface to sprout and will help to bring on a slightly earlier and heavier crop of delicious potatoes.

FRUIT

ESSENTIALS

If time is really short, try to fit these jobs in.

- **Feed and mulch fruit if not already done.**
- **Prune established currants.**
- **Prune summer-fruiting raspberries if you forgot to do this last year, then tie in new vigorous canes.**

ANY FRUIT TREES, bushes or canes will benefit from a feed right now. Sulphate of potash or rock potash supplies potassium, which helps to ensure plenty of flowers and hence fruits. Apply at 15–30 gm per square metre ($\frac{1}{2}$–1 oz per square yard) Plants take up nutrients from the soil through the finer roots, most of which are towards the edge of the root system, so make sure that you apply the feed over a good wide area – it is usually best to make this a circle – reaching to the outmost spread of the branches. A good general fertiliser will not go amiss either, particularly if your soil tends to be sandy or light.

Once the fertiliser is in place, mulch the entire area around the base of fruit plants with 5–7.5cm (2–3in) deep layer of bulky organic matter such as well-rotted manure or garden compost. Make sure that you leave the area immediately next to the canes, stems or trunks clear. This will provide a double benefit, giving the plant a much-needed general feed and increasing the fruiting potential, while at the same time acting as a mulch to help keep moisture in and weed levels down later in the season.

Regularly check that fruit-tree ties and stakes are still firmly in position and not causing any damage to young trunks. Chafing can be a problem with tree ties in particular and winter winds can cause

Growing potatoes is easy, and chitting the tubers first means heavier and earlier crops

Pruning a blackcurrant bush

Use loppers to prune out any dead, diseased and weak stems and old wood and about 30 per cent of the two-year-old stems, concentrating on lower-growing ones.

Prune white- and redcurrants and gooseberries that were not pruned in the summer (see page 101).

Prune apples and pears (see page 155), if you have still not got around to doing so. Winter pruning at some stage over the winter months is essential if you are to ensure that the plant keeps a good and attractive shape and an open habit, keep it relatively disease free and of course encourage good fruiting.

Prune back trained fruit trees (for example cordons, espaliers or fan-trained trees, or bush trees), cutting back the leading shoots on the main branches by 30–50 per cent. If the tree is not very vigorous you should prune harder as this tends to produce stronger and more vigorous new growth. If the tree is very vigorous, prune more lightly. At the same time take the opportunity to remove and dead, diseased or dying branches and, on trained trees, any overcrowded fruiting spurs.

Prune summer-fruiting raspberries if you forgot to do so in late summer or autumn (see page 101).

If you have any rhubarb growing in your garden and you want to force some particularly tender stems that will be ready a little earlier than normal, place over one of the crowns a terracotta rhubarb forcer or, if you do not have one, an upturned bucket or dustbin. The combination of the darkness and the warmth will help to produce the sticks ahead of time and ensure they are particularly tender.

Spray peaches and nectarines with a copper-based fungicide to reduce the incidence of peach leaf curl disease. Repeat two weeks later.

unexpected movement. Retighten and adjust as necessary. It is essential to double-check that they are not too tight, as a tight tree tie can severely restrict growth and will affect the tree's development and fruiting potential.

Prune established blackcurrant bushes. It is easiest to do this at this time of year, as the bare stems are not masked by foliage, so the whole task is considerably quicker. Unlike many plants, blackcurrants are able to produce fruit on both new and old wood, but to keep the plant in good shape and performing at its best, you need to remove about 30 per cent of the stems each year. Concentrate on cutting out the older stems, pruning them right back to ground level, but take the opportunity to remove any dead, diseased or damaged newer shoots in the same way. Doing this also helps to keep the bush open and so decreases the chance of diseases building up.

Sow and plant

• Provided the soil is neither waterlogged nor frozen solid, it is still a good time to plant any bare-root fruit trees or bushes or canes. Buying them in this form is usually considerably cheaper and allows you to go to a specialist fruit nursery, which will have a far better range of varieties and rootstocks than an average garden centre. When buying new fruit trees such as apples, make sure you have a suitable pollinator if necessary. Many fruit trees will fail to produce fruit if there is not a suitable pollinator in your garden or in one near by. The label should tell you which pollinator to buy, but if in doubt get help. Do not allow the roots to dry out at all before planting (see above) and when you plant, incorporate plenty of good bulky organic matter over a large area around the plant or in a good-sized planting hole. Once the new tree or bush is in the ground, apply a mulch and remember that larger trees or those on very dwarfing rootstocks may require a slanting stake for extra support.

PONDS AND WATER FEATURES

ESSENTIALS
If time is really short, try to fit this job in.

- Keep the surface of the pond at least partially ice free.
- Keep children well away from an iced-over pond.

REGULARLY CHECK THE POND surface to ensure that it has not iced over completely. A solid layer of ice over a pond surface will not only prevent oxygen penetrating but will also stop toxic gases from escaping and so can cause a lot of damage to fish or pond wildlife. With concrete ponds, and sometimes even on those with fibre glass or plastic liners, the pressure of a layer of ice on the surface can cause cracking, leading to leakage later on. If you have not taken preventative measures (see page 155), checking every few days should suffice. If the pond becomes iced over, it is essential not to smash it, as the shockwaves produced may possibly be damaging to fish or wildlife in the water beneath. Instead hold a saucepan full of very hot

PROBLEM OF THE MONTH: GREY MOULD

Grey mould (*Botrytis cinerea*) is a fuzzy grey fungal growth topped with vast quantities of dust-like spores that develops on dead or dying plant parts. It is encouraged by damp conditions and so often thrives at this time of the year. An infected plant may show browning, softening and/or dieback.

- Cut off or pick off affected areas promptly and ensure better general hygiene: never leave dead bits of plant lying around and if possible keep the atmosphere a bit drier too.
- Try to avoid overhead watering as the spores are readily spread by rain or watering splash as well as on air currents.
- Where appropriate, spray with a suitable fungicide such as carbendazim.

FIXTURES AND FITTINGS

ESSENTIALS

If time is really short, try to fit these jobs in.

- Treat timber structures if the weather is suitable, carefully removing plants first.
- Consider erecting an arch, arbour or pergola.

APPLY ANY NECESSARY wood treatments. Providing the weather is not freezing or frosty and while wooden structures such as arches, arbours and pergolas are clad in leafless plants, it is relatively easy to carefully and gently remove the plants and lay them down while you do this. Make sure that the surface of the wood is clean and dry; if necessary rub it over with some coarse sandpaper or a wire brush before you start, and make sure that it is not just about to rain. Clear algae and lichens and general debris with a wire brush if necessary. Always observe the instructions carefully to minimise the risk of any damage to the plants. You could treat wooden garden furniture too.

Construct

- This is a good time to consider putting in some extra non-living structure to your garden. Take a long hard look around and decide whether or not it would benefit from any extra height – provided perhaps by an arch, arbour or pergola. Sometimes these are available ready constructed; otherwise either build one yourself from scratch or, if time is lacking, from one of the very good kits that are around. The great thing about erecting one of these structures now is that provided the ground is not frozen you can get it up relatively quickly while there is less plant growth around and the weather is fairly cool (without your temper getting too hot!). If the weather is not frosty you

A pan of very hot water held on the ice surface melts a hole through which toxic gasses can escape

water on the surface of the ice and hold it there until it has melted a circular hole. This will allow toxic gases to escape and oxygen to enter. But do remember to hold on to the handle while the melting is in process!

If children use the garden, make sure that they are aware that an ice-covered pond is an extremely unsafe surface and if necessary block entry to the pond area. They may know that it is dangerous for much of the year, but the temptation to 'skate' can be great!

can also use any wood treatments necessary. When making any structure such as this, it is essential to think carefully before you actually erect it. Consider the types of plants you would like to grow and the conditions they need: factors such as adequate sunlight could be very important. Similarly you need to make sure that a high structure will not obscure a view that you like; and perhaps it would be worthwhile making sure that there are some scented plants already growing near by – if not, perhaps this is something else you could get on and do.

• If you want to try your hand at raising a few plants from seed and you do not have a green-house, take a look at the small pop-up cold frames and miniature greenhouses available. They may not be as attractive as a lovely timber-framed greenhouse or cold frame, but they could certainly fit the bill and will cost you an awful lot less. The great advantage of many of these is that they are also designed so that they can be collapsed at the end of the season and stored away, so there is no need for you to have them in your garden throughout the year. If small children are around, it is also worth considering the fact that many of these less glamorous options have polythene or plastic 'glazing' and so there is no need to worry about glass.

• Consider making yourself a very temporary and extremely inexpensive cold frame using old bricks, placed in a square or rectangle and raised to a height of about 30cm (12in) on the front face and about 40cm (16in) on the back face. It is essential that the sides are at slightly different heights so that the old window frame or sheet of clear plastic that you use as the lid has a camber to it, ensuring that rain will not accumulate on the surface but run off. If you then line your 'frame'

with some bubble-wrap polythene and cover the plants inside with a layer or two of fleece, they will have extra protection that should keep them snug and relatively warm, and which can be removed bit by bit when it comes to hardening the plants off.

An imposing upright structure such as an arch, arbour or pergola provides fantastic planting space and adds an extra dimension

February

For me this is a month full of excitement because so many of the spring-flowering bulbs are starting to appear. Obviously what you get depends on what you planted earlier: you may see crocuses, the first of the daffodils, a few snowdrops and a plentiful supply of stems and branches breaking into life, perhaps bearing catkins or even the first signs of foliage. But February is a mixed month and you are likely to see the coldest of the weather now too. All in all, though, it is a really exciting month because spring is definitely just around the corner.

As in the rest of winter, there is plenty you could be getting on with. Once again this is not a high-pressure time in the garden; however, there is no doubt that spending some time outside and experiencing all this early plant activity close to hand is immensely good for you – it certainly helps to cheer me up on a gloomy day – and of course any time you do spend will have great benefits later on in the year.

GENERAL TASKS

WITH TEMPERATURES potentially dropping extremely low and a fair bit of wind still about, it is essential to ensure that any plants in your garden that need protection still have it. So regularly check it, and don't forget the garden tap.

Keep feeding garden birds and replenish their water sources regularly, as water is likely to become frozen on many nights this month and may not thaw during the daytime. Recent research has pointed clearly to the fact that if you are feeding the birds (which I hope you are) you should clean up bird tables or bird feeders from time to time in order to minimise the risk of birds contracting diseases. Just scrubbing them down with plenty of soapy water and a stiff brush should do the job; or you can use special bird-feeder cleaning equipment, which you can buy from most garden centres.

Wild birds are a great bonus and many also help reduce pest numbers, so look after them!

Why not install a few bird boxes? Provided they have been properly constructed (look for those with an RSPB seal of approval) and you put them up in a suitable position, bird boxes will encourage good bird populations in your garden. If you get them in place now, the birds should have enough time to get used to them and then be prepared to move into them and use them as nesting sites. Each box should have instructions as to the best position to install it, but whatever you do, make sure that it is somewhere that cannot be accessed by cats and is in a fairly sheltered position, facing north-east if possible.

If you feel particularly virtuous and have a moment to spare, scrub out any pots or seed trays that you may be intending to use in the months ahead; this will help prevent diseases such as damping off.

TREES, SHRUBS AND CLIMBERS

ESSENTIALS

If time is really short, try to fit these jobs in.

- Cut back hedges before birds start to nest in them.
- Mulch trees, shrubs and climbers.
- Prune large-flowered clematis.
- Water trees, shrubs and climbers in containers if the weather is dry or windy; evergreens need this most.
- Plant bare-root and container-grown trees, shrubs and hedging.

IF YOU HAVE NOT ALREADY cut back hedges as you need to, you should tackle deciduous hedging now before there is any chance of birds starting to nest.

In milder areas of the country, start to prune roses, removing dead, diseased and dying stems as a first priority (see page 34). However, if in any doubt as to the weather, it is best to wait until next month.

Towards the end of the month you can prune hardy evergreen shrubs, but if there is any chance of the weather becoming particularly nasty, wait, in case any stems are damaged. The last thing you want to do is to prune a plant and then find that you lose a whole lot more of it to weather damage.

Sort out your winter-flowering jasmine as soon as it has finished flowering. If left to its own devices it is likely to form a messy bird's nest and not perform so well. Cut out all dead, diseased and damaged stems. Tie in new stems to the support system and then trim back the side shoots from the main framework of stems to within about 5cm (2in) of the main stems. The prospect of doing this may seem like a nightmare, but once

you get going you will be surprised how quick and easy it is, and it will make a huge difference to the show of flowers next year.

Brush off snow from hedges, trees and shrubs, particularly evergreens (see page 151).

Apply a general fertiliser and a good bulky organic mulch around the base of newly planted and established trees, shrubs and climbers. This will help to keep the plants growing well, and deter weeds to a certain extent, so it could save you a lot of time later in the year.

Prune large-flowering clematis (sometimes called Group 3) such as *Clematis viticella*, *C. orientalis* and hybrids such as *C.* 'Jackmannii'. Take all the stems back down to 25–45cm (10–18in) above ground level. To ensure good new growth, cut each stem back to a healthy-looking bud. Judge the extent to which you cut back by the position of

Adding mulch

A good bulky organic mulch must always be applied to moist soil, to a depth of 7.5–10cm (3–4 in) and close to but not touching the stems or trunk of the plants. It will help to encourage soil moisture retention and to keep weeds down.

Use sharp secateurs or shears to clip faded flowers on winter-flowering heathers and so keep the plant dense and floriferous

the best-looking bud. You may feel that you have massacred the plant, but this is the best way to tackle it.

Don't forget that trees, shrubs and climbers growing in containers in rain-sheltered spots may need to be watered from time to time (see page 13).

Cut back deciduous ceanothus, cotton lavender, ceratostigma, buddleias, lavatera, caryopteris and hardy fuchsias quite drastically. These all produce their best show of flowers on wood made from spring onwards, so by cutting them now, you should encourage plenty of new growth and hence flowers. Obviously if you want the shrub to get bigger, either don't do this job or just take back a few stems. In colder areas leave this job until early to mid March.

Sow and plant

• Continue to plant trees, shrubs and climbers, provided the soil is neither too wet nor too cold. Bare-rooted plants, including roses, can still go into the ground now (see page 13), again provided the soil is not frozen or extremely wet. Make sure that you prepare the soil in the planting hole well with some extra organic matter in it (use planting compost from a garden centre if you do not have your own composting system yet), and do not plant too deeply or too shallowly. If in doubt, look for the old soil/compost mark on the main stem of the plant. If the ground is at all dry, water it in well; even if the soil is fairly moist, water slightly to settle the finer particles of soil around the roots.

FLOWERS

ESSENTIALS

If time is really short, try to fit these jobs in.

- Trim winter-flowering heathers once they have finished flowering.
- Plant summer-flowering bulbs, including lilies, in beds or pots.
- Sow sweet peas.

AS SOON AS winter-flowering heathers have finished flowering, trim them over lightly, removing the old flower stems and a little bit of growth below. There is no need to use secateurs: a pair of good sharp shears will do the job perfectly and, particularly if you have a lot of heathers, make it much quicker. Trimming like this helps to keep the plants dense and should encourage better flowering the following winter.

Any of the later-flowering shrubs can be pruned now if you need to reduce their size.

Dig over the soil in any beds and borders that you want to create or add to extensively in the next few months. Avoid doing this if the soil is very wet or frozen, but as it is a job that needs to be done sooner rather than later, get going with it if at all possible. Incorporating well-rotted manure or garden compost, or even proprietary planting compost or soil improver, will help the plants to grow well.

Lift and divide established clumps of snowdrops and winter aconites that are no longer flowering well. If the bulbs of these have become over-crowded, they will not produce the number of flowers that they should. Unlike many other bulbs, they respond well to being lifted while 'in the green' (that is with all their foliage and sometimes even a few flowers on show). Before replanting, dig

Lifting and dividing congested clumps of snowdrops should mean a much better show of flowers

in some well-rotted garden compost or leaf mould and perhaps a bit of general fertiliser; then when you put the snowdrops into the ground make sure that you get them as deep as they were before. It is better to plant them slightly too deep than not deeply enough. Once you have replanted them, water the whole area in well.

Pinch out the tips on sweet pea seedlings once they are a few inches tall. Doing this will help to produce plenty of side shoots and help the plant to produce a good show of flowers later on.

Regularly deadhead winter-flowering pansies and pompom daisies as soon as the flowers fade. You may need to do this more often than you do with summer bedding, for the simple reason that really harsh spells of weather can kill off flowers. If you leave dead flower heads in place, the plant's flowering normally slows up and in addition problems such as grey mould (see page 19) are all the more likely to develop.

Make sure that any seedlings that you have been growing indoors get plenty of natural light. If they do not, they will become etiolated – drawn and leggy – and be all the more prone to collapsing or to fungal infections. If you do not have a greenhouse, keep the plants on a south- or west-facing window sill and as close to the glazing as possible during daylight hours. Standing seed trays on silver foil, or in a box lined with silver foil so that there is an upright silvery surface behind them, will also help to reflect a good deal of light back on to the seedlings, so helping to keep them good and sturdy. Crazy though it may sound, research has indicated that gently brushing the tops of seedlings does a great deal to prevent them from becoming leggy. You only need to do this a couple of times a day and

Winter aconites look stunning and bring welcome colour on a winter's day. They can be planted now 'in the green'

simply flicking over the tips of seedlings with a sheet of paper will do the job. Essentially you will be imitating the effects of natural air movement, which helps to keep stems sturdy.

Make sure that seedlings of any plants sown earlier are not overcrowded. Prick them out if necessary, taking great care to ensure that you do not damage the young seedlings.

Sow and plant

• If you want a really fantastic display of golden winter aconites or snowdrops, this is a good time to buy them, when they are supplied 'in the green' and when planted in this state they seem to establish particularly well. Once the plants have been delivered, make sure that you plant them out as soon as possible. If you cannot plant them on the day they arrive, at least open up the packaging so that the foliage does not start to deteriorate. It is essential to allow some air around the foliage, and to keep the soil around the roots so that they do not dry out.

• If you did not sow sweet peas in January, you can still do so now, but try to sow them as soon as possible (see page 15).

• Plant yourself a bit of summer colour in the form of summer-flowering bulbs, including lilies (see page 15), many of which can be bought in garden centres now. These can either go direct into beds and borders or into a few pots ready to put in a prominent position as soon as they start to put on their show.

• Early in the month sow indoors seeds of pelargoniums and other slower-growing bedding plants.

THE LAWN

ESSENTIALS

If time is really short, try to fit this job in.

- If the conditions are not too wet, prepare the ground now if you intend to create a new lawn this spring.

DURING ICY, frozen or frosty weather keep off the grass if at all possible (see page 16)

Take a sturdy old kitchen knife, a daisy grubber or a sharp transplanting trowel and dig out some of the more persistent lawn weeds – such as plantains and dandelions. Try to ensure that you get out every trace of the roots, as fragments of these can form into individual new plants. Do not compost any weeds with pernicious roots.

Using a besom or brush, distribute worm casts (see page 16).

Sow and plant

- In most areas it is really too early to sow or lay turf for a new lawn, but if you are planning to do so you can get going now. Thoroughly dig over the area, removing larger stones and any other debris. Dig out the remains of any weeds and re-rake it to remove any remaining debris or large stones. Rake and level the soil so that you have got a good surface on which to lay turf or sow lawn seeds later on. Break up large chunks of soil using the back of the rake. Obviously this work cannot be done if the soil is frozen solid or very wet, but if you get the opportunity it is a great job to do now. You will also find that if you dig over the soil and there is a mild spell, many weed seeds germinate and you can then hoe these off.

HERBS AND VEGETABLES

ESSENTIALS

If time is really short, try to fit this job in.'

- If the soil is not too wet, dig it over and fork in plenty of bulky organic matter in preparation for the arrival of this year's bean plants.

Sow and plant

- If you are planning to sow any vegetable seeds outside late this month or early next, it is worth covering the soil with cloches or a couple of layers of fleece or polythene, as this will help to prevent excess rain landing on it and keep it a little bit warmer.

- If you get a bit of spare time and have not already done so to the whole bed , dig over an area of soil, incorporating plenty of bulky organic matter, to make it ready for you to sow or plant runner beans or climbing French beans later in the year. A little bit of soil preparation like this really does make a difference to the crop you get and the incorporation of organic matter will of course also mean that the soil dries out less readily – and this will, of course, save you some time with maintenance later on. Ideally dig to a depth of about 45cm (18in) and create either a long row or a roughly circular area over which you can erect a wigwam of tall bamboo canes or sturdy sticks up which the plants can climb. By digging the trench over now you should also give the weather time to do its bit towards breaking down the soil, so improving its structure.

- Continue to sow seeds of greenhouse peppers, tomatoes and aubergines.

FRUIT

ESSENTIALS
If time is really short, try to fit these jobs in.

- Last chance to prune apples and pears before the leaves break.
- Prune autumn-fruiting raspberry canes.
- Continue to plant fruit trees, bushes and canes, including bare-root specimens.

CHECK TREE STAKES and ties (see page 12).

This is the last month you can safely carry out winter pruning of fruit trees (see page 18). Ideally if you have not already done it you should get it finished early in February. Pruning later than this may mean that you will be doing so when the trees are in growth, which is not good for them, as it can result in considerable sap loss and also increase the chances of disease.

Prune back all the canes on autumn-fruiting raspberries, taking each back to ground level. The plants will then shortly produce new canes, which will bear fruit in late summer and autumn.

If you have a good number of strawberries, pop a cloche or several layers of fleece over a few of the plants and anchor well. This little bit of extra protection will bring the crop on early and allow you to enjoy a few tasty fruits ahead of the normal cropping period.

Feed and mulch all fruit trees, bushes and canes if you have not already done so (see page 17).

Raspberry canes laden with fruit are a great, and tempting sight, and despite what you may think, they are not difficult or time consuming to grow

Sow and plant

- Continue to plant fruit trees and bushes, including bare-root specimens (see page 19).

- Plant some raspberry canes. Even if you do not have a lot of space I reckon it is well worthwhile trying to grow a few raspberries. I would always choose autumn fruiters as they are even easier to look after than summer fruiters and in my experience seem to crop well, even when conditions are far from perfect. Before planting, dig over the soil well, incorporating plenty of organic matter. If you are going to grow summer-fruiting raspberries you will need to put in place a sturdy support system on to which you can tie in the canes. However, if you grow autumn-fruiting raspberries there is no need to use a support system, so you can save yourself a huge amount of time. Each raspberry cane needs to be planted about 45cm (18in) apart from its neighbour. Make sure that you allow the roots to spread out really well. Many of the roots will be close to horizontal but this does not matter, as the new canes will develop from here. Once you have planted the canes, cut them back to about 23cm (9in) above ground level. You may get a tiny crop from summer-fruiting canes in their first year, but do not be disappointed if you get nothing. With autumn-fruiting raspberries it is not unusual to get a fair crop in the first year, as they produce their fruits on canes produced in the same year. In most gardens it is necessary to use netting or a fruit cage, or at least an extensive array of bird scarers, if you want to ensure that you are able to enjoy at least a fair proportion of the fruits yourself!

PONDS AND WATER FEATURES

ESSENTIALS

If time is really short, try to fit this job in.

- **Keep the pond surface at least partially ice free.**

REGULARLY CHECK YOUR POND to ensure that the surface does not become completely iced over (see page 19), as this can result in the build up of potentially toxic gasses beneath the ice surface and a dramatic reduction in the amount of oxygen available to pond wildlife and fish. If the surface does ice over, never break it, but instead melt a hole to allow gasses to escape and enter.

FIXTURES AND FITTINGS

TAKE THE TIME TO SCOOP out leaves and twigs from guttering on conservatories, greenhouses, garages and even your house if you can do so safely. When these become clogged with debris in autumn and winter, they soon become blocked and so do not function properly, potentially causing quite a bit of damage to the structures themselves and in some instances a downpour of water on to the soil adjacent to the building. This can cause waterlogging of any plants in the soil and can even lift small plants out of the ground.

March

Early in March it may feel as if the garden is only just
starting to come back to life after its long winter's snooze,
but even if it's making a relaxed start, that's not to say
that you can afford to go slowly. This is the month
when spring officially arrives up and down the country
and if you want to keep one step ahead of all
the action you need to be out in the garden
as often as you can.

The great thing is that I am sure you will want to get out
there, because March is one of the most exciting months
there is, and after the enforced lethargy of winter I for one
am desperate to get outside, to blow away the cobwebs
and enjoy those first magical signs of spring –
golden daffodils, and tiny new shoots and buds starting
to appear. Surely these can't help but entice you
outside and encourage you to get into gear
as the garden gets into growth?

GENERAL TASKS

GO ON A BUG HUNT. Many pests are now waking up and springing into action to attack new growth, so regular pest patrols are worthwhile. Dealing with infestations now should not only mean less plant damage but also reduce the amount of time you have to spend hunting and controlling bugs later in the year. Don't forget to look on the lower surfaces of leaves and deep within the branch structure of trees and shrubs.

Regularly hoe off weed seedlings as they emerge. You can also weed by hand, or with a trowel or hand fork, but hoeing is the quickest and most effective method. If there are any perennial weeds, try to get their roots out; with annual weeds decapitating them should do the trick. Once you have thoroughly weeded an area, a good, deep mulch may be sufficient to prevent any new weedlings from appearing. Most weeds can be composted at this time of year, but bin or burn any with pernicious or fleshy roots, or that look as if they have set seed.

It may seem harsh, but cutting back the stems of willows and dogwood like this will encourage more brightly coloured stem growth

TREES, SHRUBS AND CLIMBERS

ESSENTIALS

If time is really short, try to fit these jobs in.

- Prune roses and shrubs as necessary and then apply a general fertiliser.
- Top up or apply mulches around trees, shrubs and climbers.
- Move evergreen shrubs now if they require a new home.
- Clip overgrown ivy on walls and fences.
- Plant out newly purchased container-grown trees, shrubs and climbers.

PRUNE SHRUB AND BUSH ROSES NOW, ensuring that you cut out all dead, diseased or damaged growth and prune to a healthy-looking, outward-facing bud. These plants can be cut back hard and if there has been a lot of winter damage, or the roses were badly diseased last year, a hard prune to about 15cm (6in) above ground level should help to get them back in to shape. If you forgot to prune climbing roses back in the autumn (see page 119) you can do so now.

Prune any dogwoods (*Cornus*) and willows (*Salix*) that you are growing for their attractively coloured winter stems. Cut back to the previous pruning point or at most within three buds of this, or to a few inches above soil level, so as to encourage the production of plenty of new stems for a great show in the coming winter.

Prune *Caryopteris* × *clandonensis*, cutting last year's growth back to strong, outward-facing buds.

After pruning trees, shrubs or climbers, apply a good general fertiliser around the root feeding area and water in well if necessary.

These fiery coloured stems bring dramatic colour and structure to a winter landscape, and are easy to grow

Replace or replenish mulches around the base of trees, shrubs and climbers so that there is about 7.5cm (3in) of material (see box) over the root area but not touching the stems. The soil should be moist and, ideally, weed-free when you apply the mulch. Mulching now should help to save time later because it will help to reduce weed growth, and to keep the soil moist, so reducing the need for watering .

If you have to move an evergreen shrub to a new location, do so now when the chances of it successfully re-establishing are relatively good (see page 118).

Trim ivies that have outgrown their position on walls and fences towards the end of the month. When you have finished the area will look bare and miserable, but give the plant just a few weeks and it will produce new leaves that will mask those clipped stems. Use a yard broom or stiff brush to remove all the accumulated dead leaves and other debris that accumulates around the stems. Wear goggles to protect your eyes.

Top mulching materials
Chipped bark
Composted chipped bark
Garden compost
Well-rotted manure
Leaf mould
Chopped bracken
Cocoshells
Proprietary bagged mulch

Sow and plant

• Early March is your last chance to plant bare-root trees and shrubs (see page 13) successfully. Leave it any later and the plants will have started to break into leaf, and the amount of maintenance and aftercare will be hugely increased.

• If time is short, propagating your own shrubs may not seem feasible, but why not try layering? Many plants including mock orange, hydrangea and forsythia may even layer themselves, so look out for them doing this. To layer, simply choose a low branch that looks healthy and is growing close to the soil; improve the soil by digging in some compost or other organic matter in a small area beneath this; then cut into the lower edge of the stem at the point where it can be bent to touch the improved soil. Use a large stone to hold the stem in the soil and tie the free end of the stem to a bamboo cane to keep it upright. By next spring the new plant should have rooted and you will be able to cut it from its parent and plant it out.

• Plant newly purchased container-grown trees, shrubs and climbers. Plant up structures such as arches and pergolas now so that you can expect good growth before too long. Always tease out the roots of plants that are in the slightest bit pot-bound, if necessary soaking the root ball in water for a couple of hours to make this easier. If properly planted in a well-prepared place (with some extra organic matter or compost in it) a plant will establish better, and if you can plant before the weather heats up that vital initial aftercare in the form of regular watering will be less arduous. Firm the plants in well but take care not to compact the soil if it is inclined to be heavy and weather conditions have deteriorated.

FLOWERS

ESSENTIALS
If time is really short, try to fit these jobs in.

- Get supports for herbaceous perennials in place.
- Deadhead spring-flowering bulbs.
- Prick out and pot on seedlings as necessary.
- Lift and divide and replant congested herbaceous perennials.
- Sow hardy annual flowers including sweet peas.
- Plant summer-flowering bulbs.
- Plant out new herbaceous perennials.

GET TWIGGY PEA STICKS, canes and twine, or proprietary plant supports in place for the many herbaceous perennials that will need a bit of support to keep them looking their best when in flower. Most of these plants will only just be coming into growth this month, so it may seem premature to do this now, but done at this stage the job is much simpler and quicker and it is easier to do it without damaging the plants.

Pick off faded flowers on daffodils and spring-flowering bulbs, ideally before the seed heads start to form. This helps to ensure that energy is not wasted on seed head production, and is used instead for next year's flowers, so it will help to keep them flowering well for years to come. Leave the foliage be, or else flowering will be reduced.

Replace or replenish mulch around perennials (see page 35), making sure that you do not clog up the plant's crown and that the mulch is 5–7.5cm (2–3in) deep. Always water the ground thoroughly first if necessary, or else the mulch may end up keeping moisture out and sealing dryness in. Scattering some granular fertiliser on the soil first will encourage an even better performance.

Tidy up any herbaceous perennials that still have foliage or seed heads on them from last year. Doing this now will allow new growth to appear unchecked and remove many overwintering pests or diseases.

Prick out and/or pot on seedlings and young plants of any flowers you have sown earlier this year, handling each seedling as gently as possible to avoid damage. Watering them in with a solution of a suitable copper-based fungicide should greatly reduce the risk of damping-off disease.

Pinch out the growing tips of sweet peas sown in February to encourage more side shoots, which tend to produce better flowers.

Lift and divide overcrowded clumps of snow-drops early in the month, and replant all vigorous-looking bulbs at 3–5cm (1½–2 in) spacing and the same depth as before. Doing this should help to ensure that the bulbs do not run out of steam and fail to flower.

Sow and plant

• Towards the end of this month some garden centres start to display summer bedding plants. They may look tempting, but unless you have a heated greenhouse and are happy to care for them indoors until the end of May when they can be planted out, summer bedding is best left in the garden centre.

Prevent the flop and make it easier for yourself by getting supports for herbaceous perennials in place early in the season

Top easy-care climbers to grow over sturdy pergolas and arbours

Clematis, including *C. montana* var. *rubens* 'Freda' and *C. armandii*

Honeysuckle

Laburnum × *waterii* 'Vossii'

Rambling roses

Vitis coignetiae

Planting hardy annual seeds

1 Remove weeds and large stones, dig the soil over and then rake the soil to a fine tilth. Leave for a couple of weeks to allow weed seeds to germinate; remove the weeds.

2 Use dry horticultural sand to mark out an area for each type of seed. Uneven shapes and varying sizes usually look best.

3 Use a piece of cane or a stick to mark out the drills into which you can sow the seeds. Sowing in straight lines makes weeding much easier later on.

4 Sow each type of seed thinly in the drills and at the depth suggested on the seed packet.

5 Once all the areas are sown, carefully rake over the soil to bury the seeds, try to avoid mixing the seeds from one patch with the next.

6 Water the area well but gently to settle the seeds and provide water for germination. In a few weeks the seedlings should start to appear, the fact that they are in rows will be masked as the plants get bigger.

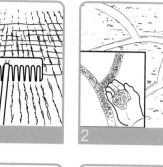

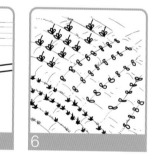

• If you want to create a fantastic splash of colour with very little money or time spent, sow yourself some hardy annuals. In most parts of the country you can do this now, but if you live in a particularly cold area, or if the soil is very wet and heavy, wait until next month. All you need is a spare piece of soil in a sunny spot and a selection of flower seeds sold as 'hardy annuals' (see box). This type of seed can be sown direct into the soil where you intend the display to be, so there is no need for compost, seed trays, propagators or pricking out. By early summer hardy annual flowers will start

to perform, and if you choose a wide range of varieties there will still be something looking good in late September or early October.

• If you have time, sow any half-hardy annuals or tender perennials to create pretty displays this summer.

• If you have not already done so, sow a few sweet pea seeds. Either sow them direct – where you want them to flower – or, if slugs and snails are likely to be a real menace, raise the plants in pots or trays (see page 15) and then plant them out once they are a few inches high and a bit tougher.

• Now is your last chance to plant winter-flowering bulbs such as snowdrops and winter aconites purchased or moved 'in the green' (see page 37).

• Plant summer-flowering bulbs and corms from the end of the month. Most garden centres should have a good selection including gladioli, lilies, montbretia, ranunculus and anemone de Caen. Check the packs for their precise needs. Remember that most of these look stunning in pots as well as in borders. Use a 50:50 mixture of John Innes and loam-free compost with added grit for containers.

• Plant out any newly purchased herbaceous perennials this month (or early next) so that they have a chance to get a bit established before summer. When choosing a new plant, always check labels thoroughly for details of the plant's potential height and spread and the sort of site it prefers. Water it in well, provide any supports needed and then mulch.

• Get some new, cost-free plants by lifting and dividing overgrown herbaceous perennials (see page 119). Provided you discard any weaker and older central sections this will also help to rejuvenate the display. Keep the new plants well watered and mulched.

• Plant out sweet peas purchased from the garden centre or sown earlier in the year as soon as the soil is not too cold and wet. Grown next to some trellis or a boring establishing hedge, or up a simple wigwam, they look great and bring trouble-free colour and perfume.

• If time permits, try your hand at propagating some pelargoniums. Choose a favourite few plants from a local garden centre now and take cuttings 8cm (3in) long. Remove the lower leaves, dip the cut end in hormone rooting powder, shake off the excess and plant in well-drained compost. The plants you raise should be in flower later this year.

THE LAWN

MAKE SURE THAT YOUR MOWER is in good working order if you haven't already done so and, if necessary, arrange for it to be repaired and serviced as soon as possible. Once the mowing

Top hardy annuals for direct sowing

Annual poppies (*Papaver rhoeas, P. somniferum, P. nudicaule*)

Baby blue-eyes (*Nemophila menziesii*)

Calendula

Candytuft (*Iberis*)

Clarkia

Convolvulus

Cornflower (*Centaurea cyanus*)

Larkspur (*Consolida*)

Lavatera rosea

Love-in-a-mist (*Nigella damascena*)

Poached egg flower (*Limnanthes douglasii*)

Rudbeckia – annual types

Sunflowers (*Helianthus annus*)

Sweet peas (*Lathyrus odoratus*)

Sweet sultan (*Centaurea moschata*)

season begins in earnest you will be amazed at how much better and quicker the job is done with a well-serviced machine.

Scarify the lawn. Even a half-hour session with a spring-tined rake (see page 125) will be time well spent and provided you get this should-best-be-done-in-autumn job done promptly, no-one will know!

Mow the lawn, setting the blades high for the first few cuts to minimise stress. If mown regularly now the grasses will grow better and denser and so should not only create a better-looking lawn but also be less likely to allow weeds to invade and spread.

Repair damaged edges and bare patches. Overseeding works well for areas of sparse grass: see page 124. Badly damaged edges can often be mended by cutting out a square of turf, including the broken area, and rotating it 180 degrees so that the damaged part faces inwards and a new edge is formed from the old inner edge. Tamp the grass down firmly so that the roots are in contact with the soil. This leaves a gap, which you can simply level up with some garden soil and re-seed with a suitable grass seed mix.

Avoid damage to edges by using a board from which to work when you are digging, weeding or planting in adjacent flowerbeds. It may take a few minutes to find something suitable, but it could save a lot of work!

Brush or vacuum leaves and other debris off the lawn now, to reduce the risk of them impeding growth. At the same time brush off worm casts (see page 16).

PROBLEM OF THE MONTH: SLUGS

Slugs, and to a lesser extent snails, can cause damage at any time of year but right now when there is a large quantity of very soft, succulent and tasty new growth they are a particular problem. Action now is therefore vital, to keep the numbers of these pests down, or at least keep them away from your prize plants.

- Look out for holes on stems, foliage and petals, combined with a silvery slime trail. Slugs do most of their feeding after dusk, so evening forays can be very productive.
- Try using the biological control nematode against slugs (if the soil is dry, you will need to water thoroughly beforehand); use traps containing beer; or create barriers with pine needles, sharp grit, cocoa shells or copper.
- Once plants have grown bigger and tougher they are better able to withstand attack.

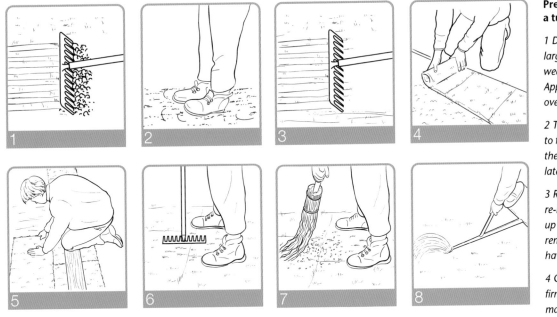

1 Dig over the soil, remove large stones, debris and weeds then rake it level. Apply a granular fertiliser over the whole area.

2 Tread the whole area to firm the soil and reduce the risk of subsidence later on.

3 Re-rake the soil to re-level it and to loosen up the surface slightly. Also remove any stones which have been unearthed.

4 Carefully roll out the turf, firming it gently and making sure each piece abuts on to its neighbour.

5 Use a plank or board to kneel on as you lay the next row of turf. Align the turves so that they are like bricks in a wall and abut each closely. Continue until all turves are laid.

6 Use the back of a rake to firm the whole area, paying particular attention to the joints.

7 Use a besom or brush to fill in any tiny gaps between the joints with sandy sieved topsoil. Re-firm edges is necessary.

8 Water the whole lawn thoroughly, re-firming joints again if necessary. Keep the turf well watered to allow it to establish.

Sow and plant

• Prepare the soil if you intend to lay turf or sow a new lawn (see page 29).

• September is the best time for sowing lawn seed, but you can also do it now (see page 125).

• Lay new turf. Although this job too can be done at pretty well any time of year, the chances of shrinkage or general poor rooting are greater if you wait until April or May, and the chances of the soil being too cold and wet are greater during the winter months. Whenever you decide to do this, it is essential that the soil is moist (or can easily be made so) but not wet and that it is not still very cold and wet. I prefer to lay turf this month as the soil is warming up and yet should still be quite moist, or at least easy to keep moist. Make sure that you order slightly more than you need and that you have chosen a suitable quality. A lawn that is very fine may require a lot more maintenance than you are prepared to put in. One with a high percentage of ryegrasses may produce a more utilitarian or rougher effect, which is perhaps great for a family lawn but slightly less ornamental. Similarly if your lawn is in shade, it may be better to go for a seed mixture or turf especially formulated to cope well with relatively shady conditions. Make sure that you know exactly when it is being delivered or when you are going to pick it up, and set aside adequate time to lay it as soon as possible, as it starts to deteriorate rapidly. As soon as it arrives, unroll it and get to work straight away. If for some reason you cannot use it immediately, unroll it and lay it on to some soil or a polythene sheet and water it gently. If left rolled up, the grasses will soon start to yellow and rot and may even die off. Bear in mind that newly laid turf must be kept really moist or else it will soon start to dry out and curl, making it almost impossible to keep the joints together; avoid doing the job unless you know that you are not about to abandon the lawn for several days.

HERBS AND VEGETABLES

ESSENTIALS

If time is really short, try to fit these jobs in.

- Regularly hoe off weeds on vegetable beds and between plants and rows.
- Dig in bulky organic matter in areas where you will grow beans.
- Plant new potatoes.

KEEP ON TOP of emerging weeds in vegetable beds. Regular hoeing between plants and rows should do the trick and will not take long. Delay too much longer and you will have bigger weeds: these will take longer to deal with, you may disturb the roots of young vegetable seedlings as you remove them and they are more likely to have caused competition as they grow. A small-headed or onion hoe works brilliantly for hoeing off weeds in small spaces.

Prepare a trench for runner beans or climbing French beans, if you have not done so already (see page 29).

Prick out seedlings of vegetables such as greenhouse tomatoes and lettuce sown under heat last month. Handle the seedlings only by their relatively tough seed leaves, never by the stem, or else you are likely to cause serious damage.

Sow and plant

- If you have time, make sowings of lettuces and cauliflower in individual cells indoors (see page 16).

- If you want to grow some unusual tomatoes from seed, or indeed if you are after a crop of aubergines or peppers in your greenhouse, conservatory, sunny porch or sheltered, sunny back yard, you can still sow seeds towards the end of this month or in early April. However, if you require only a few plants and are not worried about which varieties you grow, it is a lot quicker (and possibly also cheaper) to buy a few plants from your local garden centre during the next few weeks.

- Plant your early potatoes now (see page 17) and you should get a delicious and super-fresh crop by July. You can grow these in large containers, but you will need only one tuber per 30cm (12in) pot diameter. You will get a better crop if you grow them in open ground with about 30cm (12in) between each tuber, covered by about 15cm (6in) of soil. Allow 60cm (24in) between the rows. Place the potato so that the 'rose' or relatively blunt end (which also has the most sprouts on it) is uppermost. On poor soils digging a trench beforehand and adding bulky organic matter will increase the crop. Once in the ground

Top vegetables to direct sow now
Lettuce
Salad leaves
Endive
Peas
Spinach
Endive
Beetroot

Always obtain seed potatoes from a reputable source and, once chitted, plant as long as the soil is not too wet

this is an easy crop, and immensely good fun and rewarding to lift.

• Start sowing a few hardy vegetables (see above) direct into a well-raked soil outside, or in to large pots of compost. If you did not do so earlier, cover the soil with polythene or a few layers of fleece for a week or so before you sow, as the seeds will germinate all the sooner. Once the seedlings have emerged, a raised covering of fleece, or a polythene-covered mini-polytunnel, will help to promote rapid growth .

• Plant onion sets. Using a trowel create a hole for each so that the neck of the bulb protrudes above soil level. Don't try to save time by simply pressing each onion into the soil as this will cause compaction and increase the chances of the bulb pushing itself out of the soil as it grows. I cover newly planted onion sets with chicken wire or netting until they are well rooted to prevent birds pulling the sets out.

• Garden centres will now have a few hardy herb plants in stock such as rosemary, sage, mint and thyme. Most mints are very invasive, so grow them only in herb pots or containers plunged into a garden bed; if planted in open ground they are likely to become nightmare weeds. Get on and plant out some of these herbs now, perhaps using them as border edging, or popping them in to gaps in paved areas.

• You could make a miniature herb garden in a pot, provided your favourites are already for sale, but wait a few months and the range available will be much greater.

• Make sowings of a few seeds of hardy herbs including chives, coriander, marjoram, parsley and chervil.

FRUIT

PROTECT THE BLOSSOM of peach, nectarine or fruiting cherry trees with a few layers of fleece if practicable. With large freestanding trees it is likely to prove too difficult, but the task is much easier on those which have been wall trained.

Apply sulphate of potash to the root-feeding area of all types of fruit early this month (see page 17) if you have not done so already. You should still get a decent crop if you do not do this, but if you can spare the time now you will certainly harvest more later in the year. Make sure that you remove any mulch and then water the potash in well before replacing the mulch.

Sow and plant

• Last chance to plant bare-root fruit trees or canes (see page 19). If you want to do this, do so as early in the month as possible. If the leaves have started to break it is best to delay planting until the fruit is dormant again, or else maintenance will be a lot harder and more time consuming.

PONDS AND WATER FEATURES

ESSENTIALS

If time is really short, try to fit these jobs in.

- Remove and clear pond nets.
- Scoop out any debris which has accumulated.

CAREFULLY LIFT NETS placed over ponds to catch autumn leaves. Tip the leaves on to the compost heap or in to a leaf mould heap. Roll the netting up carefully and store it away for next autumn.

Scoop out fallen leaves and other debris that has fallen into water features or unnetted ponds over the autumn and winter. It is vital that you do this or else as the organic matter rots down in the pond it will release materials that can prove harmful to pond wildlife, fish and some plants. Once you have done this rather grotty job make a firm note in your calendar to net everything you can in good time later in the year!

Cut off any winter-damaged leaves on pond plants and marginals before they flop into the water and start to deteriorate further.

FIXTURES AND FITTINGS

CHECK THAT ALL FENCE POSTS, trellis and any other plant supports are firmly in place and structurally sound – leave this job any longer and you will have to battle with a lot more foliage and will be more likely to damage plants too, especially if you have to do any repairs.

Check, clean up and treat any wooden garden furniture, making any necessary repairs beforehand and scrubbing down seats, benches and tables – a stiff brush and a bucket of warm soapy water do a good job for all but the more delicate surfaces. Check that furniture is still up to the job

after yet another year's use. It is worth ensuring that everything is still strong enough and can bear adequate weight. This month there is often some truly stunning early spring weather and you may well want to use furniture earlier than you had anticipated.

Construct

• Put up any new trellis, arches, arbours or pergolas required for any climbers you are planting. Leave it any later than this and any damage you do to nearby plants will be less easily hidden.

An arch or pergola can be used not just to support plants, but to create dappled shade for a cool seating area

April

This month the garden really gets a loud wake-up call. Everything is putting up shoots, buds are opening and a plentiful supply of cheery flowers is bursting forth wherever you look. The added, albeit intermittent, warmth from these spring days transforms the last of the winter and early spring dormancy into a hive of activity. With an often abundant supply of rain too, combined with longer day lengths, there is no stopping the surge of growth that is April. Even if time is short and you regard yourself as a definitely-less-than-keen gardener, you will be well rewarded by each hour you spend in the garden this month.

Not only is there plenty to do and much preventative action to be taken, but I defy you to disagree that each and every minute you spend gardening this month makes you feel good too. The garden is such a vibrant place right now that you are sure to feel its vitality spreading to you, so nip outside at every opportunity.

GENERAL TASKS

APRIL MUST BE ONE of the most variable months when it comes to weather – there is usually everything from July-like summery days through to frosts (and occasionally even snow), interspersed with quite a bit of rain. This combination can mean great growing weather but it can also mean nasty and potentially very damaging shocks for plants that have been enjoying warmth and moisture only to find themselves subjected to sudden frosts. Horticultural fleece, old net curtains, cloches and even a few sheets of newspaper can often provide more tender plants with sufficient protection, but you need to get protection in place in good time, so listen to weather forecasts. Keep your eyes and ears open for signs of change, and keep plenty of fleece handy. I prefer to try to protect plants *in situ* rather than taking them into a greenhouse, and it certainly works out to be less time-consuming.

Make sure that everything has sufficient water. Despite the concept of 'April showers', this month is not always that rainy and there are often windy spells that drive moisture from the soil surface and foliage. Any plant that has been planted only relatively recently will need special care. Apply or top up mulches as necessary too.

Regularly take a few minutes to check problem-prone plants for pests and diseases. Warmer weather this month means that potential problems soon build up and, if left to their own devices, these could soon get out of hand. If you have time to do periodic general checks on other plants, so much the better. Take any necessary remedial or preventative measures promptly.

Squash, pick off, wash off or spray greenfly and blackfly (see page 64) as soon as you find them on any plants in your garden. These sap-sucking pests not only do a lot of damage in their own right but may also spread virus infections.

Pruning frost-damaged stems

Use sharp secateurs to prune out dead or damaged growth, cutting back into perfectly healthy material and to a good-looking outward-facing bud.

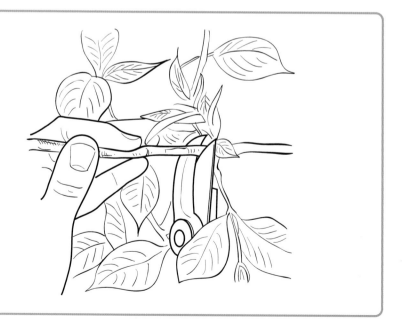

TREES, SHRUBS AND CLIMBERS

ESSENTIALS

If time is really short, try to fit these jobs in.

- Make sure that you keep anything planted within the last six months moist during dry weather.
- Prune out frost-damaged stems.
- Last chance to prune roses.
- Try to complete planting of trees, shrubs and climbers before the weather gets warmer and drier.

KEEP RECENTLY PLANTED TREES, shrubs and climbers well watered during dry weather. As they have been in the ground for a relatively short time, it is essential to give them moisture so that their roots can continue to grow and establish.

Do your own garden cost-free garden makeover. It is spring-clean time for beds and borders – rake up or vacuum up, or simply collect up the last of the autumn leaves, twigs or other debris in and around flower beds. Everything you collect, unless obviously diseased, can be incorporated in to the compost heap. Cut back or pick off any overwintering leaves left on perennials too. A tidy-up like this will not only help to remove a lot of unwanted visitors to the garden but also, within just half an hour or so, make the entire area look so much better.

Prune out frost-damaged shoots and stems. Using sharp secateurs, cut back to a good-looking, outward-facing bud or leaf. If you leave frost damage in place you are much more likely to see signs of botrytis (grey mould) later on, and this can cause shoots to die back. If there is any sign of grey mould or other infection having moved in already, cut it out completely now, before it causes further damage.

Tie in climbers and twiners to supports so that the stems are well spaced on the support and at least started off in the right direction – they will move off on their own soon enough, but get the basic shape in now and they will look much better in a month or two's time.

Give a quick haircut to lavenders, cotton lavender and curry plants. Snipping off the outer 3–4cm (1½–2in) of growth will help to keep the plants neat and compact but not prevent a good show of flowers later on. Secateurs do a great job, but with a bit of care, and then a bit of practice, sharp shears are just as good and an awful lot quicker.

Prune roses requiring an early spring prune at the beginning of this month if you did not do the job in March (see page 34).

Tie the stems of climbing and rambler roses to their supports. Aim to get as many as possible into a horizontal position as this will promote the formation of side shoots and hence more blooms. Do this promptly and the stems will still be relatively flexible and easier to deal with.

Prune forsythia and Japanese quince (*Chaenomeles*) as soon as their flowering is over. Obviously if the plants are still smaller than you want them to be, you will need to leave some stems unpruned so that the overall size of the plant can increase, but some pruning now will do a lot to encourage more flowering next year. With forsythia this means cutting the stems that bore the flowers back to vigorous new side shoots which are facing outwards and upwards. With chaenomeles cut the side shoots back to just one or two buds.

Early this month prune hardy fuchsias, *Caryopteris × clandonensis*, perovskia, *Leycesteria formosa* and *Romneya coulteri*, if you have not already done so.

If you have not already pruned dogwoods (*Cornus*) and willows (*Salix*) grown for their colourful stems, do so now (see page 34).

Consider spraying roses against debilitating diseases such as blackspot and mildew. Spraying now while infections are still slight usually prevents the problem getting out of hand, and saves a lot more work later on in the year.

Feed small trees or shrubs in containers with a controlled-release fertiliser. Gently scrape away a bit of the compost surface, scatter on the fertiliser granules and then replace the scraped-off layer with fresh compost. The fertiliser will be released to the plants gradually over the spring and summer months, ensuring that the plants are kept well fed with just a single application.

Sow and plant

• Early April is as late as I like to leave the planting of any new trees and shrubs – true container-grown plants can go in at virtually any time of year, but leave it any later than early April and aftercare and the initial establishment is likely to be a lot trickier and results less reliable.

• By planting before the weather gets too hot you will also minimise any damage caused to adjacent plants by root disturbance. Once planted, water in thoroughly and then apply a 7.5cm (3in) deep mulch all over the root feeding area.

FLOWERS

ESSENTIALS

If time is really short, try to fit these jobs in.

- Make sure all supports for herbaceous perennials are in place as needed and then apply a general fertiliser around the base of the plants.
- Continue to deadhead daffodils and other spring-flowering bulbs.
- Thin out hardy annual seedlings sown in open ground last month.
- Transplant seedlings into individual pots as they become large enough.
- Finish planting summer-flowering bulbs.

LIFT AND DIVIDE congested clumps of autumn-flowering bulbs. Replant in a well-prepared piece of ground in a suitable site for the bulb, making sure that you discard any bulbs that appear to be diseased or damaged or have been attacked by pests.

Early in the month remove any remaining over-wintered leaves on herbaceous perennials, taking the opportunity to remove any pests and diseases at the same time. Once everything is tidy, carefully rake in a pelleted chicken manure or granular fertiliser around any plants you did not feed last month. Clear away mulch before you do this, and then replace it afterwards. Take care not to drop any fertiliser on to the plants' leaves or crowns as it is likely to cause scorching.

Get supports in place for any herbaceous perennials not dealt with last month, taking care not to damage any emerging shoots.

Continue to deadhead daffodils and other spring-flowering bulbs as soon as the flowers fade.

Once spring bulbs have finished flowering apply a general feed around the whole area (whether they are growing in grass or in beds and borders), particularly those that are naturalised and in established clumps. The flowering process can use up a phenomenal amount of energy, especially if the bulbs are naturalised or multi-headed, and so applying an extra feed now is really worthwhile. This will help them to keep in good condition and flowering well for years to come. A granular general feed works well. If the weather is dry, water in well afterwards. Foliar feeding is another option and means there is no need to water in. Just water this over the foliage from a watering can and the leaves will take it up. (Or use a hose-end applicator to save time – you attach it to the end of the hose, and the concentrated fertiliser is automatically diluted to the correct level as the water moves through it). If clumps of bulbs have started to perform rather poorly or are showing signs of 'blindness' – that is they are producing good healthy leaves but sparse flowers – I would advise feeding by both methods. Doing this will save you time and effort in the longer term, as it will mean you will be able to leave bulbs for longer before lifting and dividing, and this feeding job will need to be done less frequently too.

Feed plants in containers. Because they are in an unnatural environment, these rely on that bit of extra food much more heavily than plants in beds. A liquid fertiliser is usually easiest to apply, but for larger plants in larger containers a good general fertiliser is probably the best option.

Thin out hardy annuals sown last month as indicated on the packet. This may seem like a daunting task, but take a breath and get on with it. Provided you sowed fairly thinly there may not be much to do, and all you need to concentrate on is

Pinching out the tips of sweet peas may seem like a backward step but it will mean more branching and blooms later on

removing the weaker-looking seedlings to provide more space for those with more potential. Precise ultimate spacings should be stated on the back of the seed packet, but most plants respond well to being thinned to about 15cm (6in) spacing, although some obviously require a bit more room. If you do your thinning carefully you can always transplant the 'rejected' plants into a spare patch of ground elsewhere, watering them in well. Supply a few twiggy pea sticks for taller or potentially more floppy varieties.

Prick out seedlings of any flower seeds sown within the last few weeks, handling them only by the seed leaves (these are usually the lowermost pair of leaves and relatively large and fleshy-looking). By now sturdy, good-sized seedlings will need more space and fresh compost. Never pick them up using the stem or true leaves as you can easily cause untold damage. Carefully transplant each seedling so that it is at the same depth it was previously, and then water it in gently.

Whether in borders or containers, lily bulbs planted now will help to bring colour and form later in the year

Plant out sweet peas. If you managed to sow sweet peas earlier in the year, after a period of hardening off (see page 67) to allow them to acclimatise to the colder conditions outside, the young and sturdy plants can be planted out into their flowering positions now. Applying a general fertiliser to the area will help encourage plenty of new growth.

Any small plants of tender perennials raised from cuttings taken last year should now be potted on, moving them from trays in to individual pots, to give them more space to grow and develop before planting out once the weather is reliably warmer.

Plan ahead and check out the condition of containers that you want to use for summer bedding plants next month. Discard any that need replacing and go shopping if necessary. Do this now and you should get the pick of the crop, before most people get around to it.

Early in the month prune all the flowering growth off winter-flowering heathers not trimmed earlier. This must be done now so that the plants keep their compact shape and can still produce a good display of flowers next winter, uncluttered by last year's faded blooms.

Sow and plant

• Plant the last of the summer-flowering bulbs such as *Camassia leichtlinii*, gladioli, *Triteleia laxa*, *Allium* spp., lilies, schizostylis, crocosmia, eucomis. If you plant these in good time they should provide a fabulous display on their own or among herbaceous perennials later this year, and for years to come.

• Plant up a shallow container such as a trough and create a delightful alpine display. Alpines are some of the most charming and breathtakingly beautiful smaller-scale plants, and so they are perfect for container growing.

Top alpines for growing in containers

Dianthus alpinus
Dryas octopetala
Gentiana verna, G. saxosa
Lithodora diffusa
Oxalis enneaphylla
Paraquilegia anemonoides
Phlox subulata
Primula farinosa, P. marginata
Saxifrage – many kinds
Sedum cauticola, S. spathulifolium
Thymus (creeping forms)

Planting an alpine trough

1 Choose a trough which is well supplied with drainage holes and then add a 3 cm (1¼ in) deep layer of grit to the base of the trough. This will ensure that the compost is always adequately drained.

2 Mix plenty of horticultural grit in with a suitable compost such as John Innes No.2 and then start planting. Position the pots on the surface first to make it easier to decide which plant to put where. Plant each so that it is about 1 cm (½ in) proud of the compost surface.

3 Once all the plants are in position, firm the compost and top up if necessary, water thoroughly and then top-dress the entire surface with a layer of horticultural grit about 1.5 cm (¾ in) deep.

• Introduce some movement and extra texture into your flower beds using some grasses. There are plenty of perennial grasses that can be bought and planted now; or why not sow some annual grasses from seed – a less expensive option? Most garden centres should stock a few or there will be a selection to choose from in the larger seed catalogues, including the delightfully fluffy hare's tail grass (*Lagurus ovatus*), *Eleusine coracana* 'Green Cat' (with weird but attractive green claw-like flowers), quaking grass (*Briza maxima*); or, if you want to create a mist-like effect among other plantings, try some *Hordeum jubatum*. Annual grass seed needs to be sown a little later than hardy annual flower seed, but the method is the same (see page 38). I would advise sowing in rows (to make it easier to tell your garden grasses from your weed grasses) and covering the seed to keep birds off it until it has germinated. If you do not yet know precisely where you would like to sow the grasses, you could simply use a spare piece of ground as a seedbed and then transplant the young grass plants when they are large enough to handle.

• Early April really is the last feasible date for sowing sweet peas (see pages 39 and 67).

• Towards the end of the month sow a packet or two of morning glory seeds. Soak the seeds in water for a few hours or overnight and then sow as directed on the packet. These breathtakingly

PROBLEM OF THE MONTH: WEATHER DAMAGE

Weather damage may now be noticeable on pretty well any plant. Although the injury was probably caused earlier on, now that plants are growing more strongly you are more likely to spot it. Even perfectly hardy shrubs may suffer: early and still quite soft shoot or foliage growth, for instance, will be very prone to damage and may discolour and die. Tougher leaves such as those on many trees or shrubs may show a loose or baggy epidermis (outer 'skin') on the lower leaf surface and some distortion. Provided the forecast indicates that the worst of the weather is over, you can now prune out all injured areas and wait for replacement growth.

beautiful climbing annuals produce a mass of flowers, each lasting just one day, and are a fantastic way to brighten up a trellis or create a summer obelisk of colour. Don't be tempted to sow these seeds too early as the young plants are very intolerant of cold and their growth is easily checked if planted out too early.

• Now is your last chance to sow hardy annual flower seed for a good display flowering for much of this summer (see page 38).

• Make sure that you deal with any herbaceous perennials that need to be divided or propagated by division before about the middle of this month. Leave this job any later and the new plants you create are more likely to struggle and less likely to flower this year (see March).

The combination of furry grasses and bright daisy flowers is quick and simple to achieve

THE LAWN

MOW THE LAWN REGULARLY THIS MONTH. In most years the warmer and yet moist weather means that a weekly mow is ideal and if you want to prevent the grass from becoming too long, make doing this a priority. If the weather is allowing grass to grow rapidly it can soon get out of hand, and if you allow the lawn to grow too long between cuts it will look awful when you do finally cut it. I must confess that I dislike mowing my lawn. I appreciate one that looks well cared-for but I cannot seem to put the necessary work to the top of my list. If you feel like this and have a busy schedule and some cash to spare, do not feel too bad about contracting this job out. Unless you are superhuman, you cannot do everything!

Lawns created from turf late last year or earlier this year may well need a gentle cut now too. Do this with extra care just in case the turves have not rooted completely yet.

Apply a lawn feed. Although this is not a vital job, if you want to keep your lawn looking that little bit better and to keep it growing strongly, a feed now is worthwhile. Either use a granular feed, making sure you apply it at the right rate, or else you could cause scorching. As most granular products need to be watered in during dry weather, it pays to try to time your application so that you get it on just before there is some reasonable rainfall. Failing this you will need to thoroughly water the product in when you apply it if you are to be sure to avoid scorching. Or use a liquid formulation, which can be applied with either a watering can or a hose-end applicator (see page 77).

Deal with patches of coarse grasses now. These tend to flop when the mower arrives, so escaping being cut. Try raking these coarse grasses up just before you mow. Alternatively slash the patch at 2–3cm (1in) intervals, first in one direction and then at right angles. This should keep them in check.

Sort out any remaining gaps, bumps and hollows by filling and seeding (see page 124). If left, these can make mowing difficult or cause trip hazards.

Dig out individual lawn weeds, using an old kitchen knife or daisy grubber, if there are not too many of them, and making sure you remove the root systems of those with pernicious roots such as dandelions or docks that will reappear if you remove only top growth. It's immensely satisfying when you manage to lift them out, roots and all!

If moss is still bad and you cannot put up with it, consider treating the lawn with a proprietary moss killer. Remember to ensure that you wait the prescribed time before raking out the dead moss.

Sow and plant

• You can create a new lawn using grass seed this month. For ground preparation, see page 29, and for sowing, see page 125. I find September sowings tend to work best, but if you want that new lawn sooner rather than later, get sowing early to mid-April if possible. Make sure that you choose a grass-seed mixture suitable for the type of lawn you need (see page 41).

• You can create an instant-impact lawn from turf now (see page 41), but if the weather shows signs of becoming dry, ensure that the newly laid turf is kept really well watered.

Mowing the lawn regularly means the job never becomes too much of a chore

• In some years you may need to start mowing the lawn only early this month. As soon as the grass has put on significant growth, get it cut, but with these earlier cuts make sure that the blades are set high, so that you avoid scalping.

HERBS AND VEGETABLES

ANY VEGETABLES SOWN last month may now need potting on so that they have fresh compost and a new supply of nutrients together with a little more space. Ideally give each small plant its own pot, as this will make it easier to look after and much simpler to plant out.

Protect new potato crops from frost. As soon as any growth appears above soil level it is at risk if there is frost. Mound up soil over the row, covering the new shoots as you do so. This will also help to prevent the potatoes from producing a crop too close to the surface, in which case they will be at risk of becoming green, and therefore inedible.

Keep watering any vegetables already in your garden, and those waiting to be planted out, if dry weather prevails. Remember that vegetables can be mulched to great effect. Using garden compost will have the combined benefit of providing extra nutrients as well as aiding moisture retention.

Sow and plant

- Continue to plant up herb containers or simply plant herbs in a sunny spot in open ground.

- Plant maincrop potatoes if you have the space. Although they take up much more room than early potatoes, they are great fun and easy to grow, and good for roasting, mashing or baking. Each seed potato needs to be planted, with the rose or blunt end upwards, so that it has about 5cm (2in) of soil on top of it and with about 35–38cm (14–15in) between the tubers in a row, and 70–75cm (27–30in) between the rows.

- Continue to sow seeds of vegetables such as lettuce, salad leaves, broad beans and peas direct into prepared soil. Water in well if the weather is dry. Little and often is the rule here: sow a few seeds of each every 10–14 days and you should get a good succession of crops being ready for harvest over a long period. Mark each row clearly with crop name, variety and sowing date, and make sure that part-used seed packets are kept well sealed (I use a paper clip or clothes peg) in a cool, dry place ready for the next sowing.

- If you want to try growing your own calabrese or broccoli, sow a few seeds now – preferably in individual cells, as this makes transplanting much quicker and simpler. There is no need for a greenhouse: just keep the cells moist on a window sill indoors or even in a protected spot outside. Sowing in cells rather than sowing direct outside also helps to reduce losses caused by those omnipresent slugs and snails.

- Indoors sow seeds of courgettes, marrows, gourds, pumpkins, squashes and sweet corn in the last week or so of April. There are some attractive and unusual varieties readily available now – perfect for growing with the kids or for creating your own Halloween lanterns – and you'll be impressed by the crop just one or two courgette plants can produce. On a fertile soil that is kept moist a single plant like this with its striking bright yellow trumpet flowers will look good, and produce a real feast. Other than watering, courgettes and marrows need little if any attention and are ideal to grow if you want a really easy and heavy-cropping vegetable.

• If you want to grow an unusual variety of tomato outside in a sheltered spot this year, select and sow the seeds this month. The third or fourth week in April is usually perfect for sowing in warmer areas of the country. Sow any earlier and the plants may get too leggy and drawn before you can safely plant them out. If you want only a few plants and are happy with readily available varieties, it is often cheaper and certainly a lot easier to buy plants from a garden centre when you are ready for them, once conditions are warm enough (usually in May).

• If you have a greenhouse, porch or conservatory you could consider planting a few tomato plants in a growing bag or other container towards the middle or end of the month. To make maintaining the plants easier I splash out and use cut-price bags of compost instead of growing bags. The volume and quality of compost are generally greater, and so keeping the tomatoes adequately moist is less of a nightmare.

FRUIT

MAKE SURE THAT YOU KEEP fruit trees, bushes or canes that have been in the ground for less than eighteen months moist around the roots, as they are still in their vital establishment phase. Older more established plants may need some watering if the weather is exceptionally dry, but they are not a priority.

Keep the soil around fruit trees, bushes and canes weed free if at all possible, as this will hugely decrease competition for moisture and nutrients. Regular hoeing is the quickest and most efficient method I know and once the ground is clear, it is a good idea to top it with a mulch to help to keep further weed growth at bay and encourage soil moisture retention.

Top easy-to-grow vegetables

Courgettes
Marrows
Tomatoes
Potatoes
Lettuce
Salad leaves
Climbing French and runner beans

PONDS AND
WATER FEATURES

ESSENTIALS

If time is really short, try to fit these jobs in.

- Divide overcrowded pond and marginal plants.
- Plant new pond and marginal plants and oxygenators.

CLEAR OUT LAST YEAR'S WATER from water features, if there is any still there. Scrub down the surfaces thoroughly and then rinse well to remove any traces of debris, algae, etc. before refilling with water.

Sort out older pond plants. Long-established pond plants may have grown too big for the spot you have to offer, in which case remove them from their pond baskets, divide them and then replant. You can do this in exactly the same way you would treat an herbaceous plant clump (see page 37). Discard outer or less attractive sections and use only the more vigorous-looking younger central parts. Use aquatic compost (see below), which is very low in nutrients, and dress the surface of the compost with gravel. Try to remove the container with the plants in it as gently as possible, so as to minimise disturbance of the water.

If your pond has been left untouched for many years it may need some serious attention now. April is a good month for clearing out a congested and clogged-up pond. Before doing so make sure that you carefully scoop out any fish or other creatures that live there. Always take a good quantity of pond water at the same time to minimise the shock to the creatures. Have several large buckets ready at the side of the pond before you start, each half-filled with pond water, ready to accommodate them until the clearing is finished. Bail, pump or siphon out the gungy pond water and then carefully remove sludgy mud and debris from the bottom. Do this with care in case there are any small creatures you missed earlier, and so that you do not damage the pond liner. I would not want to risk standing in a pre-formed liner; a concrete-lined pond should be a lot tougher, but remember that butyl or other flexible liners are easily punctured by the combination of a sharp stone and the weight of a human. If necessary carefully scrub out the liner before you refill the pond. Replace the plants and then when everything else is in position carefully reintroduce the animal residents with the water in their buckets.

Top plants for moist areas around pond edges

Anemone rivularis

Aruncus dioicus

Astilbe

Euphorbia palustris

Gunnera

Hosta

Iris ensata, I. sibirica

Lobelia cardinalis

Osmunda regalis

Primula denticulata, P. florindae, P. japonica

Rheum palmatum

Trollius europaeus

Sow and plant

- Fill gaps in pond plantings by introducing some new plants now. Before you buy what you like the look of, make sure that you can provide it with the depth of water it requires (too shallow or too deep can prove fatal) and that it will not become too invasive. Pond baskets make planting much easier, so choose suitable baskets for the plants you have bought. To avoid problems with high nitrogen levels, which may cause excessive algal growth, if possible buy some aquatic compost for planting up too. If you cannot get hold of any, the next best option is garden soil, taken from an area where the soil is relatively poor and has not been manured or fertilised recently. Consider using marginal plants in the very shallow water around pond edges: these not only add to the look of a pond but may also provide welcome refuges and breeding places for wildlife. If you cannot plant up everything straight away, stand the pots of new plants in a tray of water while they wait. Place each plant in its own pond basket and plant as normal, leaving a 2–3cm (1in) gap between the top of the compost and the basket rim. Cover the compost with grit to just below the basket rim – this helps to keep the compost in place and reduces interference from fish. Water each thoroughly – this also helps to keep the compost in place as you put the basket into the pond. Then carefully lower each basket into place.

• If you have had problems with algae in your pond in the past, invest in some oxygenators (plants that help to keep oxygen levels higher, which discourages algal growth) and perhaps a water lily or two to shade the water's surface. Water depth is especially important for water lilies and they need relatively still water too.

FIXTURES AND FITTINGS

CHECK AND CLEAN up garden furniture if you have not already done so (see page 45). Even a quick brush over with soapy water should work wonders.

Check that fence posts and trellis are still firmly in place and structurally sound, if you did not do so last month.

**Top marginal plants
(up to 15cm/6in depth)**

Calla palustris

Caltha palustris

Carex elata

Houttuynia cordata 'Chamaeleon'

Iris laevigata, I. versicolor

Lysichiton

Mimulus cardinalis, M. guttatus

Myosotis scorpioides

May

It really is all action this month, but there should be much to see and enjoy in your garden and lots to remind you that every bit of effort you have put in is being well rewarded – splashes of colour, lush greenery or perhaps even something tasty to eat. This is one of my favourite months because it is almost as if summer has arrived, and yet it is rare for plants to be showing any of the signs of stress that hot weather can bring.

Needless to say now that the last frost really should be over, there is plenty to do; I would describe this as one of the busiest – and most fun – months in the gardening year.

GENERAL TASKS

THE WEATHER IS LIKELY to be much warmer this month, though in many areas there is still a risk of variations and temperatures may still sometimes plummet, especially at night. It is important, therefore, to take great care when dealing with plants that are not fully hardy and those that you have given extra protection over the winter months. Allowing plants to harden off before you plant them out is definitely a good idea: wherever possible open doors and windows or remove protection during daylight hours, but make sure that it is firmly in place at night or on particularly cold days and if temperatures are forecast to fall, so as to acclimatise them gradually.

Water plants regularly during dry weather, paying particular attention to anything that is relatively new or growing in a container.

Top up mulch levels as necessary, ensuring that the mulch goes on to a thoroughly moistened compost or soil.

Weed around all plants regularly. Now that the weather is somewhat warmer, particularly if April was moist and there is still periodic rain, weeds are likely to be growing very rapidly indeed. Some particularly precocious weeds such as hairy bittercress and groundsel can grow, develop, flower and set seed in a remarkably short space of time. So 'little and often' is the rule here – far better than waiting until the weed growth is reaching jungle-like proportions and the weeds are starting to set seed. Regular weeding is much quicker and easier than sporadic weeding and also helps prevent plant competition. Most weeds can be dealt with using a hoe – with a bit of practice this is a quick and efficient method; but it is best to dig out any with fleshy or perennial roots. If you do the job regularly as soon as weeds appear you will create a lot less soil disturbance than if you try to remove larger, deeper-rooted weeds later on.

Weed in the hottest part of the day, when there is no need to remove the weeds: you can safely leave them on the soil surface, as the heat of the sun should soon dry them out so thoroughly that they wither and die, and they will also contribute to the mulch layer. If you weed just before it rains heavily, tiny weed roots often find their way back into the soil to take root again.

If you do remove weeds, unless your composting technique is brilliant do not add those with pernicious roots such as buttercups or dandelions to your compost heap. Without really high temperatures there is too great a risk that they will multiply in the heap, only to make the weed problem in your garden worse when you use the compost on the soil. Instead either bin these weeds or drop them into a large bucket or barrel of water where they can rot away. The weeds will die and then at intervals you simply use the contents of the container as a fertiliser. Likewise the seeds of weeds that have set seed can remain viable in the compost heap.

TREES, SHRUBS AND CLIMBERS

TREES, SHRUBS AND CLIMBERS that were planted last autumn or earlier this year need particular attention now when it comes to watering. It is essential not to allow the soil around their roots to dry out, as otherwise their establishment may be seriously hindered. A thorough drenching is much better than regular light sprinklings with water, as drenching allows the moisture to penetrate right down to the roots. For more on watering (see page 76).

Prune your wall-trained pyracantha to make it put on a brilliant display. Take out shoots that are growing directly away from the wall or directly into it and then reduce other shoots to about 7.5cm (3in) in length. You may feel that you have ended up with a shrub resembling a porcupine, but in fact what you have done is encourage plenty of short, flower-bearing spurs to develop, and so you will get the best possible show of both flowers and, later in the year, berries.

Prune shrubs that have just recently finished flowering. Common examples include spiraea and *Kerria japonica*. These shrubs produce their flowers on shoots that formed last year and so by pruning now you should encourage plenty of new shoot growth, which can then bear next year's flowers. Prune them by taking back the shoots that have flowered this year to buds or shoots lower down on the shrub. If the spiraea is quite old, it is also worthwhile removing about 30 per cent of the older stems, taking these right back to ground level. When tackling any woody plant, a sharp pair of secateurs is a must. Poor-quality or blunt secateurs make a rough job and you will end up spending a lot more time too as you attempt to get the blunt blades to chew through the stems. By always cutting back to a healthy-looking outward-facing bud you will ensure that the plant will stay in better shape and you will avoid having to cut out dead snags later on.

Regularly but lightly trim box, whether grown as a hedge or as topiary. Unless the job is huge I suggest using hand shears as they produce a much better end result than secateurs. It is essential to do this so that they form really good dense growth and so that you never need to cut them back hard, which they do not respond well to.

Tie in fast-growing climbers. Many climbers, in particular those that produce vigorous growth, need to be tied in regularly at this time of year: many vines, roses, ornamental hops and clematis, in particular *Clematis montana*, can soon produce too much rampant growth in the wrong place if you do not keep an eye on them. Use twine or proprietary climbing ties to encourage the shoots to grow in the right direction, but make sure that you provide plenty of room for expansion. Use ties that are flexible, as these are less likely to injure the stems, and adjustable, so that you do not have to fit new ties every time the stem girth increases.

Prune overgrown *Clematis montana* and its varieties before it takes over everything in its vicinity. Beautiful though this climber is, it has a very rampant nature and if you want to play any part in determining its ultimate size or direction you may need to act now. Prune out diseased, damaged or dead stems completely and then just trim remaining stems as necessary. If the clematis is growing through a shrub or tree, you may have to carry out extensive untangling before you can get to grips with the plant. Make sure that you tackle this job on a day when you feel full of patience! By pruning *C. montana* like this periodically you should ensure that it produces plenty of new flower-bearing growth.

Any slightly tender shrubs or other shrubs that you moved inside for winter, or covered to protect them, should be gradually acclimatised (see page 62) before you leave them to their own devices outside.

Remove bubble wrap polythene or other insulating material from around the bases of containers left outside over the winter. This can be done in early May in all but the coldest parts of the country, unless extremely hard weather is forecast.

Sow and plant

• Plant up container-grown trees, shrubs and climbers now, as early in the month as you can so that the roots have as much time as possible to get established. Remember that even if you do this, you will still have to put in more aftercare than if you had planted earlier on, or if you wait until the autumn.

PROBLEM OF THE MONTH: APHIDS

These pests – greenfly and blackfly – come in every shade, from near white or pale yellow, right through to black, with browns, pinks, greens and bronzes in between. They feed by sucking sap and in the process they may seriously debilitate plants, especially soft tender growth. They may cause puckering and distortion and in some cases discoloration. In addition, as they feed they often transmit viruses, which can cause significant damage. In some cases their sticky excreta or honeydew is produced in such quantity that the plants become sticky, as may any plants or hard surfaces beneath. There are many ways to control aphids, including two forms of biological control (best suited to aphid problems under glass), a strong jet of water directed immediately at the pests, hand squashing or picking, or a suitable insecticide. There are also products available which are especially useful for those who prefer to garden organically, including sprays based on soft soap, plant oils or plant starches.

FLOWERS

ESSENTIALS

If time is really short, try to fit these jobs in.

- Check supports for herbaceous perennials and add more if necessary.
- Continue to deadhead spring-flowering bulbs.
- Feed spring-flowering bulbs.
- Thin out hardy annuals as necessary.
- Start to buy tender summer bedding and container plants now, if you have somewhere to keep them protected.
- Plant up hanging baskets and other containers with tender plants, if you have somewhere to keep them protected.

CONSIDER RIGGING UP a temporary cold frame (see page 21), to provide extra protection for plants and help harden off tender plants that have, until now, been living in a greenhouse.

Check all herbaceous plants for signs of aphids (greenfly and blackfly), which are likely to be about right now (see page 64).

Make sure that all herbaceous and perennials that need it have got adequate support, if you didn't get round to doing so earlier in the year. For perennials with tall flower spikes such as delphiniums and hollyhocks, use an individual cane for each flower spike; it is essential that the stems are well supported or else they may snap off at the base. To support a bushier plant, you can use a system of a ring of canes and string right round the outside of it.

A cold frame need not be high-tech or expensive, but it will add a new dimension to your gardening, and make it much easier

A pair of back-to-back forks inserted in to an overcrowded clump of herbaceous perennials can be eased apart to divide the clump in to useful-sized sections

Divide large and established clumps of primulas, polyanthus and primrose. After a while these can become very congested and the rosettes can start to provide too much competition for each other. Relatively small clumps can often be teased apart by hand, but if they are too congested use two hand forks back to back and prise them apart. Cut off all dead, diseased and damaged foliage before replanting and watering in well.

Cut back and neaten up some of the earlier-flowering herbaceous perennials. Lungworts (*Pulmonaria*) and leopard's bane (*Doronicum*) are smashing plants and really valuable because they provide colour in the spring, and they can be persuaded to stay in good shape if you snip off the old flower heads and any diseased or damaged leaves. Pulmonaria in particular is prone to powdery mildew, which can make it look a real mess. By snipping the leaves off now you will also help to minimise spread of the problem. If trimmed now the plant should then produce new leaves, which will often remain in

fairly good shape on the plant right through the winter. It is also time to cut back straggly or damaged stems on aubrieta, arabis and alyssum. I love these plants, but if they are allowed to become too straggly they really look awful. Cut them back to leave just an inch or two above soil level and then give them a liquid feed. New foliage growth will appear shortly and the plants will then develop a much more compact habit. It takes only a minute to do this haircut and if pruned fairly hard each year the plants should always come back well.

Remove faded flowers from the last of the spring-flowering bulbs, using your fingers or a pair of scissors. Ideally leave the stalks in place, as these are capable of producing a fair amount of energy by photosynthesis.

Keep spring-flowering bulbs well fed (see page 51).

Continue to thin out sowings of hardy annuals made earlier this year (see page 51) and supply twiggy pea sticks for a bit of subtle support if you have not yet done so.

Remove forget-me-nots and other winter- and spring-flowering bedding plants that are past their best. With forget-me-nots if you want to ensure a good display next year, it is worth waiting until the plants have set seed and then shaking them firmly over the soil before you compost them. When the area is free of bedding plants, fork it over gently. If the soil is poor, add some fertiliser or garden compost in preparation for the arrival of the next lot of plants; however, on most soils (that is probably almost all except very light sandy soils) there should be a perfectly adequate amount of nutrients in the soil for summer bedding and herbaceous plants that follow.

Check that sweet peas are performing as they should. I often find that the plants have a tendency to grow vigorously but not always up the support provided. A little bit of winding and/or tying into the support never goes amiss in these early stages, and the great thing is that doing this also helps to keep the plants off the ground and so away from slugs. Once attached to the support in this way, the sweet peas' natural response will be to climb up it as you want them to.

Clear out any containers that have been used for winter displays. Ideally you should replace all the old compost with fresh, as recycling compost tends to lead to less vigorous plants and also increases the chances of problems such as root rots and of course vine weevil developing. When refilling containers, check that there is still a good layer of drainage material at the base. If the container, once planted, is too heavy to move into a sheltered spot and you are using summer bedding, wait until towards the end of May before planting up, or even later in colder parts of the country. If you are in any doubt about the weather, it is worth looping a few layers of horticultural fleece over tender plants to protect them.

Sow and plant

• Established or overcrowded clumps of herbaceous perennials can still be divided now (see page 38), although the new plantlets may need a little bit of extra maintenance if the weather gets very dry. Once you have planted the sections of the plant, make sure you keep them adequately moist but not overwatered, and then once they are growing strongly, apply a general feed.

Top trailing plants for growing in a hanging basket

Bidens ferulifolia
Dichondra micanthra 'Silver Falls'
Helichrysum petiolare
Lobelia
Pelargonium, ivy-leaved geranium, tropaeolum, petunia, verbena and nepeta – trailing forms
Brachyscome iberidifolia

• Treat yourself to some cheerful summer bedding plants. This is usually the best month to buy summer bedding. However, if you have not got anywhere frost free to keep the plants, I suggest you wait until the end of the month or until at least no more frosts are forecast. Plants from garden centres have often been kept in near-perfect conditions, which often err on the side of excessive warmth. It is essential to gradually harden off summer bedding plants (see below) before you plant them out, whether into containers or the border. If you have a cold frame, you can put the plants in this, perhaps with a little bit of fleece as extra protection in cold areas. During the daytime you can open the frames and then close them at night. After a couple of weeks, provided no more frosts are forecast, it should be safe to plant them out. If you have no cold frame, you can place the plants outside in a sheltered position during the day and bring them inside to a cool window sill at night.

• Plant up a hanging basket (see page 68).

Planting a hanging basket

Select a basket and bracket of matching size; smaller baskets may appeal, but as they contain less compost they dry out more quickly. Plastic-covered wire mesh lasts for many seasons, but you may choose a solid plastic basket. These dry out less easily, but you lose the opportunity of planting around the sides and unless you use a particularly large number of trailing plants it is difficult to mask the plastic basket.

1 Place your basket on a flowerpot to stabilise it and raise it off the surface slightly. The easiest liners to use and plant up are probably the recycled wool materials or cocoa fibre. Put the liner in position so that the top edge sticks up slightly above the rim of the basket. Using a sharp knife or pair of scissors, cut holes around the edges of the liner, so that you can plant through them.

2 Part fill the liner with compost to keep it in place. A standard multi-purpose compost works well (if you use this, add water-retaining granules) or you can choose one specifically formulated for use in containers, which is likely to be better able to retain moisture and easier to re-wet.

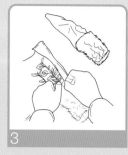

3 For the sides of the basket you can use either trailing plants or compact bushy plants. Choose plants grown in cells, as they are particularly easy to post through the holes from the outside.

4 Wrap the plants in plastic and gently squeeze the root balls to ease them through the holes, ensuring that the entire root ball is within the compost layer.

5 Top up the compost layer to cover the root balls of the plants around the edges.

6 Plant alternate bushy and trailing plants around the edge to ensure that your planting looks really dense and colourful.

7 Put an upright plant in the centre of the basket. Nestle it into the compost and ensure that the top of the compost the plant is in is level with where the compost in the basket will be.

8 Fill in with planting around the remaining ring of empty compost. Top up compost levels if necessary. When planting around the edges take a minute to ensure that you have not planted next to the anchorage points for the basket chain. If you have, move the plants as otherwise they are likely to be decapitated as soon as you hang up the basket. Water the basket thoroughly but gently, using a watering can with a rose attached.

68 **MAY**

THE LAWN

- Apply a spring lawn fertiliser if not you did not do so last month.
- Last chance to repair bare patches in lawns.
- Mow regularly.
- Control lawn weeds by hand or by using a chemical lawn weedkiller.

APPLY A SPRING LAWN FEED – it is not too late to do so if you did not get around to it last month (see page 54).

Continue to repair thin or bare patches in the lawn and crushed lawn edges (see page 40). It is better to get as much of this done before the end of May, as any repairs tend to 'mend' quicker before the weather gets too dry.

Continue to mow your lawn regularly. In most areas grass will now be growing fairly strongly, particularly if there has been some rain, so you should be able to gradually lower the blades to decrease the height of the cut. If you are in any doubt about the speed at which you should be lowering the blades, it is always better to delay slightly and leave the lawn a little too long, rather than risk scalping it – that is, cutting it much too short. A scalped lawn not only looks awful but – particularly if a period of dry weather follows – may take quite a while to recover, and you may be unlucky and find that bare patches develop where the grass was cut too short.

Control weeds. If you have just a small lawn, or more time to spare than usual, you could cut out individual weeds or small patches of weeds (see page 55). If you are happy to use chemicals, there is no doubt that for a larger lawn or for a heavier weed infestation the quickest way to control weeds is to use a selective or broad-leaved weedkiller specifically formulated for use on lawn weeds. A product that contains a fertiliser and weedkiller combined is your best option as you can do two jobs with one application. Make sure that you apply the product at precisely the rate stated on the pack: too little and it may not have the desired effect, too much and it is possible it will scorch off the weeds without killing them properly and in some instances perhaps scorch the grass. Ensure that you apply chemical weedkillers only during suitable weather conditions, taking especial care to avoid using them when the weather is even the slightest bit windy or gusty, or very hot and sunny. Tiny amounts of weedkiller can easily drift on to flowerbeds and borders and do a lot of damage.

Give a first mowing to lawns grown from seed earlier in the year. Once the individual blades of grass are 5cm (2in) or slightly more in height, it is time for that first trim. You must set the mower blades as high as possible and go gently. If there are any signs of the grasses being pulled out at the roots, either the mower needs sharpening or you may need to wait a little longer. As time progresses you can gradually lower the blades to cut the grass slightly shorter, but always err on the side of caution.

Sow and plant

- May is the last chance to sow a lawn from seed (see page 55) without a huge amount of aftercare. If you sow any later, conditions tend to be much drier and warmer and you will need to do an awful lot of watering – unless, of course, you wait until the autumn.

HERBS AND VEGETABLES

HOE OFF OR GENTLY HAND FORK out weeds in and around crops. Hoeing is not only generally quicker than hand removal or forking out, but disturbs only the surface of the soil and does not affect the roots of the crop plants.

If you are growing any carrots, cover the seeds or developing seedlings with horticultural fleece, fixed firmly in place at all points. This will help to prevent carrot fly damage, and so you should not need to experience any unpleasant maggoty carrots.

Regularly and thoroughly water vegetable crops, especially during dry weather, and once the soil is moist, consider using a good bulky organic mulch to help the soil to retain moisture and to keep weeds at bay.

Continue to mound up the soil along rows of early potatoes. If growing conditions are good, you may need to earth up later potatoes too, at least twice this month.

Regularly remove side shoots from tomato plants. At least once a week you will need to spend just a few minutes carefully breaking off the tiny side shoots as they develop and tying the plant in to its support if necessary. Simply grasp the side shoot firmly between your forefinger and thumb, holding it towards the base. Then bend it down sharply and snap it off, leaving no traces of it on the main stem and so drastically reducing the chances of any infections developing. If you leave removal of the side shoots for too long the plants will crop less well and the job of removing them will take much longer because of the jungle-like mass of stems and foliage. Removing large side shoots also increases the risk of injuring the plant itself.

Sow and plant

- Sow indoors seeds of French beans, runner beans, courgettes, marrows, sweet corn and pumpkins into cells or small pots. If you keep the cells or pots on a sunny windowsill the extra warmth there will make a huge difference to the rate at which the seeds germinate and the young plants grow. In most areas the plants should be ready for planting out towards the end of May or early June. I prefer to sow inside and then plant out, as this reduces the amount of losses caused by slugs and snails.

- Direct sow seeds of runner beans, climbing French beans, French beans, sweet corn, courgettes and marrows if you are worried that you would not be able to keep a close eye on young seedlings in pots (see above). Check the seed packets for precise sowing depth and distances, as these vary slightly from variety to variety as well as from crop to crop. Once watered in, seeds grown outside can usually fend for themselves slightly better than those in relatively small pots or cells; however, there is a greater risk of slug or other pest damage.

- Towards the end of the month, or early next month, plant out any courgettes, marrows, French beans and sweet corn plants that you have raised

Regular removal of side shoots on tomatoes makes the job easier and you are less likely to damage the plant

have a nasty habit of turning an unpleasant purply yellow colour and then refusing to 'move' for weeks on end. Far better to wait and make sure the conditions are a little warmer.

• Create some productive pots by planting up larger containers with sweet pepper, chilli pepper, aubergine or tomato plants. If grown in either a good quality multi-purpose compost or 50:50 mixture of multi-purpose loam-free compost plus a loam-based compost, and if kept well watered and fed with a high-potash fertiliser, these pots can be amazingly productive when placed either in a very sheltered and sunny spot in the garden, or in a porch, greenhouse or temporary clear polythene shelter. Do not risk placing any of these plants outside until all danger of frost is passed and ideally cover them temporarily with a clear polythene sheeting shelter, fleece or similar material until the middle of next month. This should ensure that the plants continue to develop well and perhaps even start to form a few flowers.

yourself or bought from a garden centre. Harden off the young plants thoroughly before planting out; and if you are in any way concerned about ups and downs in temperature, particularly at night, cover the plants with a few layers of fleece held loosely in place with a couple of bricks. Water the young plants in thoroughly as soon as they have been planted out and if the weather happens to be hot, try to do your planting out in the early evening, so giving the plants the rest of the evening, night and early morning to settle in and take up some moisture before being subjected to the heat of the day. If necessary, erect some temporary shading for the first couple of days.

• If you have a sheltered garden in a relatively warm part of the country, or at least a sheltered spot, you could start to plant outdoor varieties of tomato now (having bought plants at a garden centre). However, if in any doubt, it is always worth waiting until next month before you do this, as if planted out the slightest bit early, young tomatoes

Vegetables that do well in containers

Aubergines
Chilli peppers
Courgettes
French beans
Herbs
Potatoes (earlies)
Radishes
Runner bean 'Hestia'
Salad leaves and lettuces
Sweet or bell peppers
Tomatoes

FRUIT

ESSENTIALS

If time is really short, try to fit these jobs in.

- Raise developing strawberries off the soil, using mats or straw, and check for pests.
- Water fruit as necessary, replenishing mulch if need be.

CUT OFF RUNNERS DEVELOPING on established strawberry plants, using a sharp knife. This is essential as runners tend to weaken the main plant. If you want to use the runners to create new plants, pot them on (see page 87).

Place proprietary strawberry mats or handfuls of dry straw beneath small fruitlets on strawberry plants. This helps to ensure good air circulation around the young fruits and so greatly reduces the risk of grey mould developing. It also keeps the fruits slightly off the ground and so reduces slug and snail damage. As you get the mats or straw in position, check the base of the plants carefully for slugs and snails and remove these. Strawberries growing in planters will not need mats or straw, as their fruits tend to dangle in mid-air. However, it is still worth checking all parts of the pot for any slugs and snails that may be lurking there.

Make sure that you keep all fruit trees, bushes, canes and other fruit plants well watered, particularly if the weather is dry, and don't forget to top up bulky organic mulches to ensure that the soil remains moist.

Prune fan-trained plums and cherries from the middle of the month – any time until early August. If you are lucky enough to have a fan-trained tree, it is really worth taking the time to keep it in shape, as this will not only make it look

A trained fruit tree can look beautiful and it also allows you to grow fruit in a relatively restricted space

much more attractive but also help it to keep its shape and to fruit much more prolifically. Start by removing any shoots that are growing either away from the framework or directly in towards the wall. Next remove crossing shoots and thin out any that are overcrowded. You also need to remove any damaged, dead or diseased stems, in each case pruning back to a healthy-looking bud facing in the appropriate direction. The shoots that remain can then be tied into the wires.

Sow and plant

• Early in the month plant container-grown fruit bushes or trees, but remember that autumn planting means less aftercare and, generally, quicker establishment.

PONDS AND WATER FEATURES

ESSENTIALS
If time is really short, try to fit these jobs in.

- Clear blanket weed and duckweed.
- Plant new pond plants.

THIN OUT OR DIVIDE any pond plants that have become a bit too big for the positions they occupy (see page 58).

Clear blanket weed and duckweed from your pond or water feature. These weeds both grow extremely fast and so it is essential to keep on top of them, just as you would with weeds in a flower bed. By drawing an old sieve carefully across the pond surface you can quickly scoop up much of the duckweed. If blanket weed is a problem dip a sturdy bamboo cane in to the centre of the algal mass, twist it around a few times and you will be amazed at how much algae you pull out each time. Don't waste time with a flimsy cane: the weight of a mass of water-soaked algae is more than you might imagine and will snap a thin cane easily. Done regularly this job does not take long and is immensely satisfying, but if you leave the weeds to get out of control, it can be really difficult and time consuming and pond plants are likely to suffer. Leave the blanket weed or algae in a place to dry out in the sun and to allow any pond wildlife that you might have scooped out to return to its home, and then add it to the compost heap.

Sow and plant

• Take a critical look at your pond and see if it needs any more plants, as it is easier to plant now than it is any later in the year. For choosing and planting (see page 58).

June

Everything is on the move right now, and there is a lot to do. The weather has reliably warmed up and so plants are growing fast. This is a really exciting time of year as you become surrounded by lush greenery and a good display of early summer flowers. But there are problems: weeds are growing even faster than your garden plants, and the lawn is racing to create a jungle. Pests and diseases are rearing their heads and breeding or spreading rapidly, too.

This is one of those months when it is well worth dedicating a bit more time to gardening than you did at the beginning of the year, because if you don't it will all too easily start to get the better of you. But now that the evenings are longer and warmer, grabbing a hoe, a trowel or a fork should seem more appealing. It is still early enough in the growing season for you to catch up on jobs which you didn't get around to before, and you should find that any late sowings or plantings will soon make up for lost time.

GENERAL TASKS

IDEALLY YOU should have mulched in late April or May, but if you do this early in June, the results will be nearly as good, reducing the need for watering and weeding. The soil is still relatively moist now, so before the weather gets any warmer, mulch anything that needs it (see page 35) and replace or top up mulches around the bases of plants if necessary. Leave this job any later than early this month and shrubs, climbers and trees in particular may already have had to put up with quite a bit of competition from weeds, and with drought stress.

June is often very dry and if your soil is light and free draining, or if the weather is particularly dry, watering will be one of the main jobs this month. Plants are all the more likely to suffer if allowed to get dry. Fast-growing plants will be particularly thirsty. Anything that has been planted relatively recently is likely to need more attention in the form of regular thorough drenchings than well-established plants. Some flowers, especially annuals, need a good deal more water than others, and if they are allowed to become dry now their flowering potential may suffer.

If the ground is already very dry, sprinkle the soil or compost surface of all the areas to be watered, before doing the proper watering a few minutes later, once the sprinkled water has penetrated. This first dampening moistens the surface and reduces the amount of water lost by surface run-off. Water really thoroughly, rather than just watering the surface of the soil. This allows water to get right down to the roots and should mean that you have to water much less frequently. Remember that for best results and least wastage, water once the sun has gone down, when possible; if you've had a really stressful day cooped up inside this 'chore' can become a pleasure and be very relaxing. Failing that, water in the early morning. Watering in the heat of the day is not only more likely to cause scorching of the plants, but also wastes water because so much is lost by evaporation – and so takes longer because it is less effective. Aim to keep the soil just moist beneath a surface layer that is likely to be dry.

If you have several plants in one area it is worth considering setting up a porous hose system, to ensure that the ground is kept just moist at all times. These pipes are readily available from garden centres, and can be laid around the plants, covered with mulch or a thin layer of soil and then allowed to seep water in to the soil – saving a lot of watering time.

If the watering of containers is a bit of a chore, try grouping them together – that way the pots will heat up less and the foliage will loose less moisture, so less watering will be needed. You can also reduce watering by placing a pot of flowers below a hanging basket as the pot will enjoy the run-off from the basket above. When you feed the basket with a liquid feed, those beneath will also share in the meal too.

If you have a lot of containers it may well be worth considering an irrigation system. This need not be complex or pricey; for instance, a small trickle irrigation system can easily be linked up to a whole patio, terrace or balcony full of pots. Such a system can save an immense amount of time and ensure that the plants never suffer the effects of drought.

With luck you will have mulched some weeds out of existence, but any that do appear you will need to deal with speedily (see page 62).

Most plants are growing and developing rapidly now and so will benefit from a good general feed. A good early-summer meal helps to promote further new growth and in many cases, plenty of flowers. It also sets up most plants for the next few months without promoting soft and frost-susceptible growth too late in the year (although overfeeding can cause problems). Most summer bedding in containers is planted up in early to mid-May and so by June much of the fertiliser content of the compost has been used up. Give a good liquid feed now and you should prevent even the slightest check in flowering.

Plants vary in their specific requirements, but you can save time by using a high-potash liquid fertiliser to feed a range of plants including summer bedding, tomatoes and herbaceous perennials. Anything that can be applied using a watering can is quick and easy. Although such a fertiliser tends to offer only a very general feed, it will certainly help to perk up most plants. At this time of year I give most flowering plants such a feed regularly. The high potash content helps to encourage more flowers and so is especially useful for summer bedding. If you use a tomato fertiliser, you can use the same feed for flowers, tomatoes, peppers and aubergines. A hose-end applicator is a useful way to apply both food and water in one fell swoop (see below). If you use a dry or granular fertiliser, apply it just before it rains, when there will be no need to water it in. A feed like this needs to be applied once a week or more, unless you have used controlled-release fertiliser granules in the compost. Even if you have, I would still recommend feeding with a high-potash fertiliser every ten days to two weeks, as the high potash content encourages more flowers.

Unfortunately June weather is very pest- and disease-friendly, so you will need to check regularly for potential pests and pathogens. By doing this you will be able to avoid disasters. A good time to make a quick inspection of the plants is when you are watering, feeding, planting or otherwise caring for your plants – that way checking will not take you any significant amount of time. The soft young growth on herbaceous and annual flowers makes a particularly tasty meal for pests, so concentrate on shoot tips and always investigate curled leaves. As most pests and diseases spread incredibly rapidly, prompt action is your best line of defence. You can often stop a problem in its tracks, so saving time (and plant distress) later on. Picking off or squashing an early attack may mean that little or no more action is needed later on, and avoid the need for chemicals. If you decide to use pesticides, always ensure that you choose one that is recommended for use on the plant you have in mind and also that it is suitable for controlling the specific pest or disease your plants are being troubled by. Spraying in early evening is advisable as it reduces the risk of scorch damage occurring on the plant and of inadvertently harming any beneficial insects such as bees.

Hose-end applicator

A hose-end applicator is easily attached to the hose and if the hopper is filled with a suitable fertiliser the feed is automatically diluted to the correct strength as the water flows through.

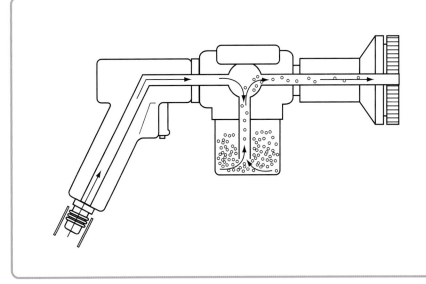

TREES, SHRUBS AND CLIMBERS

ESSENTIALS

If time is really short, try to fit these jobs in.

- Water recently planted trees in dry weather.
- Feed woody plants.
- Look out for aphids on soft new growth.
- Remove suckers from roses.
- Tie in new growth on climbers and wall shrubs.
- Prune out any frost damage.
- Prune and dead-head spring-flowering shrubs.

WATER RECENTLY PLANTED TREES in dry weather. Once they are established, most trees, shrubs and climbers will perform well despite a good deal of dry weather, but those planted within the last year or two will benefit from a weekly drenching during dry weather.

Feed woody plants. A good general fertiliser (see page 34) will benefit many woody plants, but try to finish feeding by the end of this month. Feed later and you may stimulate soft growth that may not be adequately hardened off before the first frosts. Some of the plants that start to initiate flowers this year for a display next spring may also abort their buds if fed too late on. Camellias are particularly prone to this.

Look out for aphids on soft new growth. Soft new growth on trees, shrubs and climbers is likely to be being colonised by pests, in particular aphids. To deal with these, see page 64.

Remove suckers from roses, if your roses have produced suckers from their rootstocks – now, rather than waiting until they have become a thicket. Suckers usually have a slightly different leaf shape and a paler colour. If possible, pull the sucker off close to the root of the parent rose.

Tie in new growth on climbers and wall shrubs to the support system promptly (see page 63). At this time of year the stems are much easier to deal with because they are more flexible and pliable, and should not yet have become entangled with each other.

Shrubs to prune in June

Buddleia alternifolia
Chaenomeles
Cotoneaster (deciduous)
Deutzia
Exochorda
Kolkwitzia
Philadelphus
Ribes sanguineum
Spiraea
Syringa
Weigela

Prune out any frost damage if any of your shrubs, trees or climbers were damaged by late frosts earlier on and you have not yet dealt with it. It's important to tackle them now, before secondary organisms such as grey mould or coral spot colonise the stems and cause more severe and more time-consuming problems. Cut back damaged branches to a healthy, outward-facing bud.

Prune and deadhead spring-flowering shrubs. Some shrubs that might not have finished flowering until now will benefit from being pruned this month. This will encourage new shoots to develop and these will then produce flowers next year. June is your last chance to cut back excessive growth on *Clematis montana*. Overgrown lilacs can be cut back hard now. If otherwise healthy they should regrow well if cut back to just 45cm (18in) or so above ground level. If you can spare the time, remove the faded flowers from camellias, rhododendrons and lilacs, but if it is not possible, don't loose sleep over it – I have known plenty of such plants which have never been deadheaded yet perform brilliantly year after year.

Sow and plant

• You can still plant container-grown trees, shrubs and climbers this month, but remember that they may need intensive aftercare, in particular watering, if the weather gets dry.

• Propagate climbers such as clematis by layering.

FLOWERS

TIDY UP spring-flowering perennials. Remove damaged or diseased leaves and faded flowers.

Cut off or tidy up discoloured and fading foliage on spring-flowering bulbs. You can now safely do this without jeopardising their next year's flowering potential. If you leave deteriorating leaves in the border they may encourage slugs, and the flopping foliage of naturalised bulbs in grass and makes mowing even more time consuming.

Lift naturalised spring-flowering bulbs such as daffodils in grass and separate and replant congested clumps to reduce the risk of them failing to flower properly in future years.

Mark bulb clumps. If you are planning to do any major planting later in the year in an area that already contains bulbs it is a good idea to use markers to indicate the location of the main clumps of bulbs. Come autumn there will be no

Herbaceous geraniums can be kept as beautiful and compact as this if given a haircut as soon as the last of the flowers have faded. This may also encourage a second flush of flowers later on

Thin out hardy annuals that are still too closely packed. Hardy annuals sown in spring may still need thinning (see page 51) early this month. Leave it too long and the stems of the young plants will become drawn and possibly entangled with each other, which makes thinning really tricky and time consuming, and means that many plants will get damaged. After you have thinned out the plants, water the area. This will resettle the soil around the roots, making them less likely to suffer from drought. This should be the last thinning – check seed packets for 'final planting distance'.

Start deadheading late spring and summer-flowering plants. From this month on you will need to spend some time removing faded flower heads from summer bedding and herbaceous perennials. By pinching them between finger and thumb or cutting them out as soon as they fade, you will conserve the plant's energy and reduce the risk of diseases such as grey mould infecting the faded flower and then damaging the rest of the plant. Removing faded flowers will prevent the plant from forming seed heads and help to ensure that the plant produces more buds and flowers later on.

sign of the bulb foliage and you could waste a lot of time replanting bulbs you have mistakenly dug up and then re-digging planting holes – so get markers in place now.

Lift spring bulb baskets, if you grew spring bulbs in plunged baskets last autumn (see page 124). Place the baskets in a sheltered spot where the bulbs can die back out of view.

Continue to add supports to herbaceous perennials with easily damaged flower spikes, before the flower stem gets snapped off. This job is best done earlier in the year, but if you have not done it already, it is not too late (see page 36).

Trim geraniums and alpines. Some of the earlier-flowering herbaceous geraniums may have finished flowering by the end of this month. Although their foliage is attractive, it is worth giving the plants a good haircut now, using a pair of shears – the ultimate in quick deadheading technique. This may feel brutal, but by clipping off the faded flowers and a little bit of the adjacent foliage you help the plants to remain bushy and in many cases they will produce a second flush of flowers later in the summer or in early autumn. You can use a similar quick technique for many rock garden plants (alpines) that have finished flowering, and for aubrieta. For these a sharp pair of scissors is perfect for the job.

Pinch out shoot tips on summer bedding. A lot of summer bedding requires pinching out if the plants are to remain good and bushy, or in the case of trailing plants if they are to produce some side branches and not become too straggly. It is much quicker and simpler to do this now than wait until next month when there will be a lot more growth to deal with and the plants will already have lost some of the opportunity to produce side stems. Prompt action also reduces the risk of plant damage.

Sow and plant

• You can safely plant out tender plants such as bedding and tender perennials this month, provided you harden them off first (see page 67), although in the very coldest areas of the country you may need to wait until the middle of the month. I prefer to get these planted in late May (see page 67); however, if the weather is at all variable by waiting until this month to plant them you reduce the risk of plant damage and will not need to be running in and out with fleece or other forms of protection for them. To allow these plants to establish more easily and to save time on aftercare, mix up a 'slurry' of water and soil, place generous quantities of this in each planting hole, position the plant and then use dry soil to finish off the planting. The cap of dry soil will help to keep the roots and their planting slurry moist for longer. Retain more soil moisture by mulching, but avoid bark-based materials which may stress these relatively delicate plants.

• Early June is the best time to plant up summer containers and hanging baskets if you do not have a greenhouse in which to grow on plants in containers before displaying them outside. For planting details, see page 68. When you've planted up a container, leave it in a sheltered spot for a week or two before positioning it in its long-term home: a bit of pampering at this stage makes for a better end result.

Top ten plants for summer hanging baskets

Begonias
Busy lizzies (*Impatiens*)
Fuchsias
Geraniums (ivy-leaved)
Helichrysum petiolare
Lobelia
Pansies (*Viola* x *wittrockiana*)
Pelargoniums
Petunia
Verbena

PROBLEM OF THE MONTH: POWDERY MILDEW

Dry soil conditions encourage powdery mildew infections on pretty well every plant. A white, powdery coating on leaves, and sometimes on stems and flowers too, is often accompanied by distortion, yellowing and dieback or defoliation. At this relatively early stage in the growing season a severe attack of a powdery mildew fungus can cause quite a lot of damage. Options for prevention and control include:

- keep plants adequately moist at the base but also try to encourage good air flow around the top growth by avoiding overcrowding, keeping adjacent weeds cleared and where relevant careful pruning;
- consider using resistant varieties, where available;
- pick off/prune out infected areas and collect up any fallen infected leaves;
- consider spraying with a suitable fungicide, where available.

• Early this month is your last chance to sow hardy annuals (see page 38). If there is bare earth in between plants in your beds, fill them: hardy annuals not only add colour – rows of sunflowers or lower-profile splashes of colour look great – but also help to swamp out many weeds which would otherwise colonise those gaps. Hardy annuals that should still flower reliably when sown now include godetia, calendula, sunflower and candytuft. The drier soil conditions now should mean slightly fewer slug losses, but will also mean more watering.

• Herbaceous perennials should still be readily available in garden centres this month and should establish well, but these relatively late plantings will need a bit more watering and general care than those planted in the spring or autumn. For these too a mulch is essential if you are to save time on watering and weeding.

• Sow inside in pots or trays seeds of herbaceous perennials such as hollyhocks, alpine poppy, oriental and Iceland poppies, lupins, achillea, anchusa, aubrieta, *Centranthus ruber*, delphiniums, *Digitalis* spp. erigeron, campanulas and geum. You may get some flowers later this year but most of these plants will perform best next year.

• Sow inside seed of winter-flowering pansies and polyanthus for colour early next year.

• Sow seed outside of biennials such as forget-me-not, sweet William, Brompton stock and wallflowers for colour next spring.

• Spring-flowering herbaceous perennials such as primroses and primulas can still be divided (see page 66), early this month, but remember to keep the new plants well watered during dry weather.

• Root 10cm (4in) cuttings from favourite pinks. Non-flowering shoots should root well in pots of sandy compost in a cold frame.

THE LAWN

ESSENTIALS

If time is really short, try to fit these jobs in.

- Water in dry weather, if the lawn is new.
- Mow the lawn regularly.

IN VERY DRY WEATHER, water your lawn occasionally but thoroughly. If you laid a new lawn from turf or sowed one from seed earlier in the year it is essential that you keep it well watered in these early stages (see page 41).

Control lawn weeds. Some people like to see a few daisies in a lawn and are not thrown into despair by a bit of moss or a patch of clover, but if you aspire to a closer-to-perfection lawn, this is the month to get to grips with lawn weeds. The quickest method is probably to use a lawn weedkiller chemical (see page 69).

Feed the lawn if you did not do so in the spring. If you just want to give the lawn grasses a bit of a boost and feel there is no need for weed control, this is still a good time to apply a lawn feed. You can soon give a somewhat tired and miserable lawn a bit of a facelift with the application of a fertiliser now. There are lots of different products available, but remember that by choosing a liquid feed you can save yourself a job because there will be no need to water it in. Use a fertiliser appropriate to the time of the year. Probably the simplest way to apply a lawn feed is via a hose end applicator (see page 77).

Mow the lawn regularly. Mowing is something that you need to do frequently at this time of year. If the mower is not performing as it should, get it serviced, fixed or replaced without delay. For most lawns setting the blades fairly low – at 1.25cm (1/2in) or slightly higher – should ensure that the lawn looks good. Provided that you cut the lawn regularly and the clippings produced are small you can save time by allowing the mower to redistribute the clippings back out on to the lawn where they will act as a mulch, providing protection against drought. If you don't mow often enough the clippings will be longer and so should not be left on the lawn. The decision is yours! If you have a lot of lawn clippings to dispose of, mix them with plenty of drier material such as prunings before adding them to the compost heap. If you don't you will have a very smelly, slimy mass of rotting grass.

Use edging shears to neaten up the lawn edges. Even a family or utility lawn can be made to look a lot smarter by edging it. It is easiest to achieve neatly trimmed edges quickly if you tackle them once a week. The trimmings can go on to the compost heap. Edging may seem time consuming, but it can have such a dramatic effect on the overall appearance of your garden that it is worth the effort.

Reseed if necessary. It is still possible to reseed or overseed bare or thin areas on an existing lawn (see page 40), but the seed and young grasses will need regular watering.

HERBS AND VEGETABLES

ESSENTIALS
If time is really short, try to fit these jobs in.

- Water in dry weather.
- Weed in and around all fruits and vegetables.
- Feed tomatoes.
- Take precautions to minimise pest problems.
- Plant out tender vegetables.
- Remove side shoots from tomato plants.

WATER IN DRY WEATHER. I try to avoid using water unnecessarily in my garden, but fruit and vegetables will produce much better results if given adequate water during hot or dry weather. Crops such as lettuce (which is prone to going to seed or bolt if allowed to get dry), peas and beans (which without water simply fail to set pods) and cauliflowers (which do not produce a decent head) should be top priority. On any soil it is worth remembering that all fruit plants benefit from a mulch and that most vegetables will thrive if given a good bulky organic mulch shortly after planting.

Weed in and around all fruit and vegetables. If you are growing a plant for its crop it is perhaps all the more important not to let weeds take the lion's share of moisture and nutrients from the soil. Among smaller crops such as lettuce, weeds also tend to cause a localised increase in humidity around the crop leaves, and this is likely to encourage many diseases such as mildews, rusts, grey mould and leaf spots. So if you can't keep plants weed free, at least make sure that you weed frequently enough to ensure that the weeds don't get too big.

Feed tomatoes. Crops such as tomatoes, peppers and aubergines need regular feeding at this time of year.

Take precautions to minimise pest problems. You will need to control or prevent the many potentially damaging pests around at the moment wherever possible. By checking plants on a regular basis you should be able to catch most problems in the early stages (see page 64). If, however, you get pests on your crops, and there is a suitable chemical to control them with, use it if you wish. I prefer, though, to garden organically, particularly when growing fruit and vegetables. Wherever possible it is worth creating a physical barrier to prevent pests from reaching your vegetables. You can keep a crop of lettuce, rocket or Chinese leaves, for instance, clean as a whistle by covering the young plants with a fleece or fine horticultural mesh. It will take a bit of time to get this sort of barrier in place, but once there it will prevent many pest problems. No need for several different chemicals or to spend time reapplying a pesticide. This sort of barrier works very well for pests such as aphids, caterpillars, root flies and flea beetles. If slugs are a real problem it is still worth applying the biological control slug killer (and see page 40); remember that if the soil is dry, you will need to water thoroughly beforehand.

Plant out tender vegetables you have been raising from seed since earlier in the year such as sweet corn, courgettes, marrows, pumpkins, squash, climbing French, dwarf French and runner beans. As long as you have hardened them off properly (see page 71) there should be no need to provide them with protection. If the soil is dry, water it first before planting or put a 'slurry' of very wet soil in the planting hole.

Plant out tomatoes into the garden. When you do this make sure that the plants are watered in well and ideally plant them in early evening so that they are not immediately subjected to any high temperatures that may occur during daytime.

Support your beans. Nothing is more disheartening than to see plants develop a good crop only to find much of it is ruined but a few twiggy sticks driven in to the ground at intervals amongst dwarf French beans should prevent them flopping on to the soil and getting damaged or slug-infested.

Carry on removing side shoots from tomato plants (see page 70).

Start to harvest early potatoes. Choosing a dry day drastically reduces the amount of soil that adheres to the tubers on lifting. If you are unsure whether the plants are ready, simply expose the young tubers at the base of one plant and check their size and quantity. If they are still very small, you will probably decide to wait a week or two more before lifting another plant, but even marble-sized new potatoes are delicious, so don't let them go to waste. Remember that the foliage on new potatoes does not need to be yellowed before you start to lift the crop.

A container filled with favourite herbs looks great and if positioned close to the house, is convenient for cooking too

Sow and plant

- You can still direct sow courgette or marrow seed into open ground or a good-sized container.

- You can still direct sow gourds, squash and sweet corn.

- By all means sow yourself (straight into the ground) some interesting and tasty lettuce or salad leaves but bear in mind that if it is very hot the seeds will not germinate so you'll not get a lot for your efforts. In very hot weather sow the seed in a partially shaded spot and germination will be quicker and better. To avoid too much wastage from slug and snail damage choose varieties with a purple or red colouration to the leaves.

- Sow Chinese vegetables such as Chinese leaves and pak choi.

- Plant up a container of herbs, if you haven't done so already, and put it close to the back door for easy access when you are cooking. Choose a selection of herbs that you actually enjoy using in your cooking.

- Make sure that the soil is really moist and keep a watch out for slugs and snails.

FRUIT

ESSENTIALS

If time is really short, try to fit these jobs in.

- **Thin out fruits on apples, pears and plums.**
- **Erect props to support limbs likely to bear an excessively heavy crop.**
- **Raise developing strawberries off the ground on straw.**

THIN OUT FRUIT on apples, pears and plums. If you have a well-established and thriving plum, apple or pear tree that is inclined to produce an excessive crop, you may well have witnessed the damage that an exceedingly heavy weight of fruit can do as it breaks the branches. A minute or two spent thinning the fruit out slightly this month can prevent such damage and still leave you with a fantastic yield. Start by picking off any young fruits that are showing signs of damage or a pest or disease attack. Then later this month or early next, once the natural 'June drop' or thinning has occurred, you may need to take a few more. Don't be tempted to do too much thinning before nature interferes, or you may be left with less than you want. If you wish to have fairly good-sized apples or pears thin further as necessary, so that there is about 10cm (4in) between each fruit. If you are less concerned about fruit size – and indeed with some of the larger fruiting varieties you may prefer to have a higher quantity of smaller fruits – thinning is obviously much less important.

Erect props to support limbs likely to bear an excessively heavy crop, if you feel there is a risk of damage. Set up a sturdy prop now, resting the susceptible branch on it. Make sure that the branch is resting on a surface that will not cause abrasion or other damage.

Layering a strawberry runner

1 The runners formed around a strawberry plant are potential new plants. Remove any which are unhealthy and leave just enough for the number of plants you wish to form.

2 Improve the soil beneath the mini plant on the runner. Carefully plant the mini strawberry and water in well. A U-shaped piece of wire helps to keep the runner in position and prevent the planted from being dislodged.

3 Once the new strawberry has formed a good root system cut it off from the parent plant and plant it out, then tidy up the parent.

Prune plums, cherries, nectarines and almonds. Any pruning that has to be done on these trees is best done this month or next as this limits the risk of silver leaf (see page 72.)

Raise developing strawberries off the ground with straw if you did not do so in May (see page 72).

Regularly check strawberries and remove damaged fruits as these increase the likelihood of grey mould developing.

Continue to harvest rhubarb sticks until the end of June – after which point they tend to become excessively stringy.

Sow and plant

• If you need a few new strawberry plants and your existing plants are healthy, peg down a few runners using a U-shaped piece of wire. Ideally pinch out all but the plantlet or two closest to the parent plant, as those closest tend to form better plants. You can do this straight in to the soil or, better still, peg the runner into a small pot of compost which you plunge in to the ground. This may be a bit more fiddly now, but it makes it much easier when it comes to lifting the plant later on.

PONDS AND WATER FEATURES

CONTINUE TO CONTROL duckweed or blanket weed on a regular basis (see page 73).

Consider introducing barley straw. A bright green pond can often turn quite clear if you submerge a fine-mesh bag full of barley straw in the water. A pair of old tights makes a great 'bag' for the straw and can then be weighted down using a few bricks. If you cannot obtain barley straw, it is possible to buy ready-made 'pads' of suitable straw specifically for clearing algae from ponds.

Make sure that water levels are maintained. Occasional topping up may be necessary in order to maintain plants and wildlife during hot weather.

Sow and plant

- June is a good time to introduce new surface-floating plants to a pond. At this time of year surface floating plants should establish well and quickly, and even those that are a bit tender should do fine. The great thing about plants that float on the surface of your pond is that they not only look good but also serve a great time-saving purpose: whatever they are – an elegant water lily or an exotic water hyacinth – these plants will provide some shading of the pond surface, which helps to keep algae in check. So floating plants reduce the risk of your pond turning bright green or becoming clogged with the filamentous alga, blanket weed.

FIXTURES AND FITTINGS

WEED AREAS of hardstanding. Areas such as terraces, patios or gravelled paths may need weeding. Even tiny weeds popping up through cracks between paving slabs or finding their way through a gravel area will soon get a hold and start to set seed. Where weeds are growing in these places I usually find that easing them out by hand, perhaps using a hand trowel, is the easiest method; or a flame gun works well. For larger areas you may decide to use a suitable weedkiller. This will almost certainly prove quicker than hand weeding, but remember to ensure that there is no risk of contaminating nearby garden plants. Applying a weedkiller with a dribble-bar attachment on a watering can is quick and easy and makes it simpler to direct the chemical just where you need it.

Make new areas of hardstanding. If you decide to put down paving or gravel, take that bit of extra time with preparation. If the area is heavily infested with pernicious weeds, consider using a systemic weedkiller before starting the job. This should kill off the weeds, roots and all. A relatively or, better still, completely weed-free area beneath the hardstanding can save you a lot of time and irritation later on. Bedding paving on to sand without any mortar makes life easier for weeds, and harder for you. Mortar between the slabs should keep weeds out. If you are putting down gravel, it is essential to lay good-quality membrane material on the levelled and compacted soil surface before you put the stones down. Although not completely foolproof, this material will go a long way towards stopping most weeds from coming up and appearing through the gravel. It may be a bit of extra work and expense initially, but the time it can save later is phenomenal.

Sit outside. June is the month when you really start to get more use out of garden furniture. You may well have brought it out of hiding last month, but now, with regular sunshine, you can get to sit outside more often. Apart from the occasional wipe-over the furniture should need little if any attention.

Control ants. You may need to attempt to control ants now on areas used for sitting, eating and drinking. Use a proprietary ant killer or carefully apply boiling water to the nest.

An area of hardstanding can help to create a year-round place to eat or catch the sun

July

July is when your garden is likely to be looking at its best, with wonderfully colourful displays in flower borders, pots and other containers. If you have managed to squeeze in a few vegetables, many of these should now be cropping heavily. Because the weather is, generally, a good deal warmer now and days are longer, there are many opportunities to enjoy your garden in later afternoon and early evening.

You might take this to mean that there is also to be a lot of work to do, but, to be honest, this is not one of the most time-consuming months in the garden, which is great because it means you have all the more time to enjoy the fruits of your labours. However, if you want to keep the garden looking as good as it can for as long as possible, you still need to carry out a fair amount of maintenance work and to keep your eye on plants and their problems, just in case anything tries to get out of hand.

GENERAL TASKS

A simple trickle irrigation system may be the answer to watering problems, and will save a lot of time

THIS IS USUALLY ONE of the warmer and drier months of the year, so it is essential to keep those plants that need it adequately watered. In hotter weather you may prefer to do quite a bit of the gardening work towards the end of the day, or perhaps even early in the morning when temperatures are cooler, and these are also the best times to water the garden. For the best way to water (see page 76). Make sure that as much as possible of the water is retained in the soil by applying or re-applying to the moist soil a good bulky mulch.

If you are going on holiday, make sure that you ask a friend or neighbour to pop in and keep containers (see below) or other higher-maintenance plants adequately watered. If you have a greenhouse or conservatory, regular attention will be vital if the plants are not to suffer.

If you have not already installed at least one water butt, make sure that you do so now. Admittedly at this time of year there is unlikely

to be a great deal of rainfall, but you should try to collect as much rainwater as possible. Also consider installing a water diverter to take 'grey' water such as bath water and water from the shower or hand basin. This can then be collected in one or more water butts and used as a brilliant source of moisture for garden plants. However, I would advise you not to use water collected from the outflow of either a washing machine or a dishwasher, as these are likely to contain too many salts and/or chemicals and so could prove harmful to certain plants, and may possibly cause some environmental damage too.

Water diverter

Install at least one water butt and use a water diverter fitted into the downpipe from the bathroom, or from the roof guttering. Diverters are available in various sizes and shapes to suit most drainpipes.

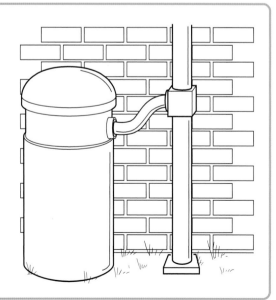

TREES, SHRUBS AND CLIMBERS

ESSENTIALS

If time is really short, try to fit these jobs in.

- Check for pest and disease outbreaks.
- Make sure you have someone lined up to keep an eye on your plants and their watering if you are going on holiday.

Ensure good dense growth on conifer hedges by pruning them now (see page 107). Relatively new hedging needs to be cut back regularly so that it establishes a very dense and yet leafy structure.

Cut back the long whippy growths produced on wisteria towards the end of this month, or early in August. You need to take them back to within about six buds from the main stem. This can be a time-consuming job, particularly on a large plant or one that is growing high up a wall or over a pergola, but it is essential to do it now, as it will encourage plenty of flower buds to form, ready for a good display next year.

Prune larger-leaved evergreens this month too. Spotted laurel (*Aucuba*) and laurel (*Prunus laurocerasus*) should, ideally, be treated to a trim using secateurs. This method takes an awful lot longer than using a powered hedge trimmer but will ensure that you are not left with an ugly array of tattered and roughly cut-through leaves. If time is short (or if you simply find a job like this extremely boring) you could tackle your hedge in stages, interspersing this less-than-inspiring task with other more interesting work in the garden. Doing this will also reduce any muscle weariness or strain.

Using sharp secateurs, remove blooms from roses as soon as they fade. Cutting right back to a bud in a leaf axil should help to ensure that the plant

retains a good shape and continues to flower as late as possible into the year. If you really want to save time and you have a lot of roses you could prune with a hedge trimmer; research has indicated that this method is actually very efficient – though I for one hate the look of the rather ragged stems that result. Remember to leave faded roses on any plants which you are growing for their autumn hips. These will include many of the wild roses and also others such as *Rosa moyesii* 'Geranium'.

A good high-potash fertiliser will help to encourage strong winter-hardy shoots and general good growth on roses, and a plentiful supply of flowers. Ideally you should use one formulated especially for use on roses. This is not a difficult or time-consuming job and applied now and watered in well, the fertiliser will hugely influence the appearance of the plants next year.

Removing faded roses promptly helps to reduce disease problems and keep the plant performing well

Taking semi-ripe cuttings

1 Choose a healthy shoot of this season's growth and cut if off just above the node. Avoid any diseased or damaged stems.

2 Use a sharp knife to remove the side shoots, then trim back the main stem just below a node to leave a cutting 10–15cm (4–6in) long.

3 Remove the lowermost few leaves and then cut out the very soft growth at the tip of the cutting.

4 Dip the base of the cutting in hormone rooting powder, tap off the excess and place each cutting in a pot of cuttings compost in a cold frame or propagator. Once well rooted, pot into a larger individual pot and harden off before planting outside.

Cut out any growth that is appearing at the base of trunks of trees or shrubs, using sharp secateurs. If left in place these will grow rapidly and soon start to draw energy away from the main body of the plant, so it is essential to cut them out promptly and close to the trunk.

Prune early summer-flowering shrubs such as weigela and the mock orange *(Philadelphus),* using sharp secateurs. Ideally this should be done early in the month. It will help to encourage plenty of new flowering growth for next year.

Sow and plant

• If you have the time, consider creating a few plants for free by propagating some of your favourite shrubs. This is also a great way to get unusual varieties of shrubs that you have seen in gardens belonging to friends and neighbours. At this time of year new stems on many shrubs are starting to harden up and become woodier and so the type of cuttings you take are known as semi-ripe (see step-by-step illustration). If you use a large pot you can place several cuttings in it, but make sure that the leaves of one do not touch those of its neighbour. Water lightly so that the compost is just moist, place a clear polythene bag over the top of each pot to act like a mini-cloche, and then position the pot in a shady spot in the garden. This may sound quite complicated, but once you have done it you will find it is actually quite easy; and about two months later when the cuttings have rooted sufficiently to be potted on, the sense of achievement you'll get will be worth that little bit of time investment!

Shrubs for propagating using semi-ripe cuttings

Aucuba
Berberis
Carpenteria
Ceaonothus
Cotoneaster
Elaeagnus
Escallonia
Lavender
Photinia
Pieris
Rhododendron
Skimmia

FLOWERS

- Deadhead annuals, perennials and roses to help the plants to continue flowering for as long as possible.
- Make sure that all containers are kept adequately moist.
- Pick flowers such as sweet peas and dahlias to make more come.
- Prune early-flowering shrubs.
- Cut flowers for drying such as lavender, statice and everlasting helichrysums.
- Plant autumn-flowering bulbs as soon as they become available.
- Make sure you have someone lined up to keep an eye on your plants and their watering if you are going on holiday.

DIVIDE OVERCROWDED and congested clumps of rhizomatous iris. Once they have been in your garden for a few years, these types of iris start to get congested and will not perform as they should. So, using a garden fork, carefully lift each clump and then, with a sharp knife, divide the rhizome into separate chunks, ensuring that you use only very healthy and vigorous-looking material and that each clump you create has a few roots and some leaves attached. You may feel that you are massacring a previously reasonable plant, but once the deed is done you will see how much good you have achieved. Strip away any dead or damaged leaves and then, using the sharp knife, cut the remaining foliage back to leave about 15cm (6in). You now have a selection of small, potentially vigorous iris plants, which should immediately go into a well-drained soil in a sunny site. Make sure that you plant the

rhizomes so that the very top surface of each is just peeking up above the soil. It is essential to trim back the foliage as this will help to prevent the plant being moved about by wind and so allow the rhizomes to root more easily.

Continue to regularly and thoroughly deadhead annuals, perennials and, if possible, shrubs (see page 79). If you find deadheading tedious and time-consuming, remember that it is much easier to do small amounts of it regularly than to set yourself too huge a task in one go; regular deadheading will also be better for the plant. Always carry a pair of secateurs with you while you are doing other gardening tasks and then you can snip out the odd faded flower. Try to spend at least a couple of minutes every few days removing the faded flower heads from summer bedding plants in containers or in open ground.

Take a pair of scissors to hardy geraniums (see page 80). Giving this type of plant a 'haircut' now helps to keep them good and compact, and in many cases will also encourage a second, later show of flowers towards the end of summer or into autumn.

Take every opportunity to check plants for pests or diseases, as the relatively warm weather tends to make many of them increase quite rapidly. Dealt with promptly, these are much easier to control and it is less likely that the plants will be seriously damaged.

All containers need much more regular and heavy watering than plants growing in open ground. All the faded flowers can be added to the compost heap and this close inspection of the plants will also allow you to check for any outbreaks of pests such as greenfly and blackfly which are likely to be very troublesome at this

time of year. If you find keeping container plants (in hanging baskets, wall baskets, window boxes, pots and other containers) adequately watered is taking up too much time, it is well worth considering installing a simple trickle or drip irrigation system. These are nothing like as expensive as you may think and it is often easy to install a system simply for your main containers, making watering while you are at home a lot easier and completely solving the problem of garden watering if you are away on a summer holiday. Alternatively, if you are going away, and have asked a neighbour or friend to water containers for you at least once a day, if the pots are relatively small you could even persuade them to 'adopt' them for the period of your holiday. (If possible ask them to do a bit of deadheading, as even over a period of a week or two summer bedding plants left with faded flowers on them can start to wind down their flowering.) If you are away just for a long weekend, it may be worth moving baskets and other smaller containers from sunny positions to a shadier spot, where they will be much less likely to dry out so fast – it is amazing how much difference this will make to the rate at which the plants lose moisture. It may be sufficient to thoroughly drench the compost in containers.

Pick flowers such as sweet peas and dahlias as frequently as you can. If you are off on holiday for a week or two ask a neighbour to come in and help themselves. Picking will not only provide you or your neighbour with a wonderful array of gorgeous blooms for your house, or to give away to friends, but will also mean that these plants carry on flowering better and for longer.

Cut flowers for drying now. Cut lavender just before the buds open fully, when the stems have not just been wetted and tie them in loose bunches before hanging them upside down in a well-ventilated, warm spot. If you have grown flowers such as statice or other everlastings, most of these should now be ready for drying.

As with lavender, you should always try to pick the blooms before they are completely open and certainly before there are any signs of any of the flowers deteriorating. Cut the stems as long as possible and tie them into small bunches before hanging them upside down in a well-ventilated shed, garage or room.

Regular feeding with a high-potash liquid fertiliser is essential for containers of summer bedding, especially since it is likely that you will have placed these in very sunny spots in the garden.

Sow and plant

• As soon as columbines (*Aquilegia*) have ceased flowering and formed ripe seed heads, pick off a few and sprinkle the seed in an empty part of the garden where you could do with a little bit of extra colour next year. They germinate and grow incredibly readily and need little, if any, care, so are a wonderful way to fill gaps.

• Bring some beautiful shapes and colour to your garden in autumn by planting some autumn-flowering bulbs and corms such as colchicum, nerines and autumn crocus. Most garden centres have these available from this month and if you plant them now you will be able to enjoy the elegant lilac, pinkish purple or white flowers for much of the autumn and for years to come. All these plants prefer a sunny and fairly sheltered spot and it is essential that drainage is good. If you are at all worried about the drainage on the site you have in mind, dig in plenty of grit before planting; you could even add some extra grit to the base of each planting hole. These plants look fantastic planted in rough grass or on a sunny bank, or perhaps even as a mini-naturalised drift beneath a favourite tree or shrub or planted in amongst herbaceous perennials. Colchicums or naked ladies, as their common name suggests, are striking plants that produce their flowers before the leaves appear. I think they look best planted in untidy grass on a sunny bank; or they can look great as a small drift beneath favourite shrubs or trees. When the leaves are produced in the spring, they take up quite a bit of space, so make sure that there is other plant growth there to detract from them.

Top ways to keep containers happy in summer

Choose bigger containers as they dry out less readily.

Before planting line the sides of the pot with bubble-wrap polythene to insulate it.

Incorporate moisture-retaining granules in the compost at planting.

Group pots together to help to keep them cool.

Mulch the compost surface to preserve moisture.

Keep plants well fed with a high-potash feed.

Deadhead regularly.

Check for pests and diseases.

Keep them really well watered.

THE LAWN

MOW YOUR LAWN once or maybe even twice a week and you will find the job easier and that the end result looks a lot better. If there has been rain and warm weather these will have stimulated grass growth amazingly, so regular maintenance is essential. The mowings will be quite short, in which case you can leave the collecting box off the back of the mower as the cuttings will help to act as a mulch. However, this month tends to be dry, in which case you can afford to let the grass grow slightly longer, as this will make it better able to cope with any drought conditions. Cut with the blades slightly higher (with the collecting box on the mower) – that way you are less likely to damage the grass in the long term.

Providing the ground is not too dry, apply a liquid feed to your lawn to give it a bit of a boost (see page 111).

Keep recently laid or sown lawns well watered at all times. Older, established lawns, should however be left to their own devices if at all possible, as even if they start to show signs of browning or deterioration because of dry weather they almost always recover perfectly well once wetter weather sets in. If you do need to water the lawn, use a sprinkler (see page 76) and water in the evening, or failing this very early in the morning before the temperature rises.

PROBLEM OF THE MONTH: ROSE BLACKSPOT

About the only good thing about this fungal infection is that it can only attack roses, so no other plants are at risk. However, it causes a phenomenal amount of damage on almost all roses and so you need to take it seriously. Purple/black blotches develop on the leaves and may coalesce in extreme cases. Rapid and premature leaf drop results and so this infection can have a seriously weakening effect on the plant.

- Regularly and promptly rake up infected fallen leaves to reduce the risk of the disease being carried over to the next year.
- When you do your early spring pruning (usually about March) make sure that you prune out any stems bearing tiny purple/black markings as these often allow the disease to be carried over from one year to the next.
- Consider spraying with a suitable fungicide, but if you do choose this route, make sure that you get give the treatment straight after the March pruning and then carry on at the suggested intervals, as inadequate or incorrect spraying is rarely of any use at all.

HERBS AND VEGETABLES

GARLIC BULBS should be ready for lifting when the foliage starts to yellow. If you want to enjoy an unusual and very tasty garnish for salads or soups, lift a garlic clove before the foliage starts to yellow and chop the green leaves finely – they are delicious. Use a fork to gently lift the bulb from the ground and then leave it on the soil surface if dry, or on a path or old pallet, to dry off for the day. This will ensure that the bulbs store well.

Onion sets planted last autumn should also start to become ready from this month. They are ready for harvesting once the foliage flops and yellows. Use a garden fork to gently loosen each bulb from the soil and then, once the foliage has dried off completely, lift the bulbs and dry them off. I use an old pallet as this gives really good air circulation beneath, but if you are growing smaller quantities of onions, a piece of chicken wire lifted off the ground will do as well.

Make sure that you keep tomatoes, aubergines and peppers well watered and fed with a liquid high-potash fertiliser. Tomatoes and peppers growing in containers may need watering at least twice a day if they are to continue to grow well and you are to avoid the fruits developing blossom end rot (black leathery patches on the flower end of the fruits). Peppers and aubergines and even the occasional greenhouse tomato plant may start to fruit so heavily that there is a serious risk that stems will break, in which case the crop will be lost and the plant damaged. It is worth popping some sort of mini-prop beneath stems that are obviously under stress.

Regularly remove side shoots from tomatoes in order to prevent the plants from becoming too wild and bushy and to keep the growth and vigour centred around the developing trusses of the fruit (see page 70).

Keep all vegetables adequately watered (see page 84). This is one area of the garden where I use water more readily as if you allow cropping plants to dry out, they often run to seed or bolt and so are useless. Concentrate your efforts on crops such as lettuce and brassicas, which are more inclined to suffer drought stress. Runner beans – and to a lesser extent climbing French beans – can be a complete failure if they are not kept adequately moist. If necessary add a mulch around the base of the support up which the beans are growing, but make sure that the soil is really well watered before the mulch goes on.

Pinch or cut out the tip of the main, leading shoot of climbing French or runner beans as soon as reach the top of their supports. This will help to encourage more side shoots to develop lower down on the plants, which should give you a bigger crop.

Trim back exuberant growth on herbs using sharp scissors. Take special care to remove any flower heads: this will help to keep the plants growing well and give them a good dense shape. Any herb cuttings that you cannot use immediately can always be chopped up and frozen in ice-cube trays. Part fill the ice-cube tray with water, top up with chopped herbs, then add a little more water. The end result tastes a lot better than if you try to dry your own herbs.

Continue to lift and eat early potatoes (see page 85). Depending on the variety, the location of your garden and precisely when you planted the seed potatoes, you may only be enjoying your first crops now.

In colder parts of the country you may have to leave planting out tomatoes into the garden until early in July (see page 85).

Sow and plant

• Make sowings of salad plants such as lettuce, rocket, claytonia, lamb's lettuce and even beetroot now. If you want larger plants, try to sow the seed fairly thinly, but if you prefer baby leaves you do not need to worry about thinning at all and can simply snip off the leaves as and when they are of a suitable size. Sowing in rows makes it easier for you to see where your crop plants are and will make weeding much easier. Keep the seedbed and subsequently the young seedlings watered to ensure good germination rates and steady growth.

• Carry on sowing oriental vegetables such as mizuna and pak choi for use in stir-fries or as interesting additions to salads later in the year. You could buy a packet of mixed Chinese vegetable seeds – this often works out more economical if you only have a small area.

• Plant up a container of favourite herbs if you have not already.

Many of the oriental vegetable crops are simple to grow and, like this Mizuna, are great in salads and stir fries

Top quick-and-easy salad crops to sow now
Claytonia
Rocket
Lamb's lettuce
Lettuce
Pak choi
Mizuna
Oriental spinach
Spinach
Olive-leaf wild rocket
Chinese cabbage
Purslane

FRUIT

ESSENTIALS

If time is really short, try to fit these jobs in.

- Prune summer-fruiting raspberries as soon as they finish cropping.
- Prune established redcurrants, white currants and gooseberries towards the end of the month.
- Support potentially overladen branches on fruit trees.

PRUNE SUMMER-FRUITING raspberries as soon as you have enjoyed the last of the crop. This is likely to be towards the end of July, but will depend on what varieties you are growing. Cut the canes back to ground level, ensuring that you remove only those which have borne fruit this year; leave the more flexible and greener canes in place. The canes that need removing are usually pale brown and noticeably sturdier than the new canes. Before you start brandishing your secateurs, untie the old canes from the supporting wire. Prune the canes that bore fruit last year back to ground level and then cut them free from the support system. It is easier to do the pruning first and then cut them lose as the canes will be held neatly in place for you and not be falling down around your ears! Once you have done this take a long hard look at the new, green canes that were produced last year but which did not bear fruit and prune out all but seven or eight, leaving only those which look healthiest and most vigorous. Tie them on to the support with garden twine so that they are about 10cm (4in) apart. Any stems that are taller than the top of the support system should be bent round and tied in, as this helps to encourage good fruiting in the summer.

Use sharp secateurs to remove the old canes on raspberries once fruiting is over

Towards the end of the month prune established red currants, white currants and gooseberries. First remove all dead, diseased, damaged or crossing shoots, together with any that are growing towards the centre of the bush and making it congested. Trim all the side shoots made this year back to three or four buds from their point of origin. Pruning fruit for the first time will take you much longer and seem more nerve-racking than it will after a few attempts, but it will be time well spent as it will ensure good air circulation around the stems and so greatly decrease problems with pests and diseases. It will also allow more fruit buds to form and the fruits should ripen more readily because of the extra sun they receive.

When fruit trees are heavily laden it is worth supporting the branches with a prop to take some of the weight and prevent breakage

time of year strawberry leaves can look quite a mess and getting these discoloured leaves out of the way now will help to minimise disease problems. If you have just a few plants do this by hand or with a pair of scissors. If you have quite a lot of strawberries give them a haircut with a pair of shears to leave just the leaf stalks; this may look rather drastic but if you do this towards the end of July it should have little if any effect on the vigour of the plants and it is certainly a lot quicker than removing the leaves individually. As soon as the tidy-up is complete, take the opportunity to clear thoroughly between the rows, removing old straw and any weeds that may have appeared. Keep the plants adequately watered in dry weather and within a few weeks you should see new and completely healthy-looking leaves appear. Any plants which have performed very badly this year and are old should be removed completely and then replaced later on.

Prune plums, cherries, nectarines and almonds if you didn't do them in June (see page 72).

Thin out the fruits of apples and pears – they should have finished their natural thinning out of fruits now (see page 86).

Install a prop beneath particularly heavily laden branches of well-established fruit trees (see page 86).

Remove discoloured, damaged and diseased old leaves from strawberries. Whether the plants are growing in open ground or in a container, by this

Sow and plant

• Peg down runners on strawberry plants to create new plants (see page 87) if you did not do so earlier.

• Any strawberry runners that you pegged down into the ground or into pots of compost last month should now be ready for planting. With those in pots, carefully check the root system and if it is well developed it is time to sever the plantlet from the parent and plant it up. If the weather is extremely dry or the plant seems not to have rooted that well yet, you can wait until next month.

PONDS AND WATER FEATURES

ESSENTIALS

If time is really short, try to fit these jobs in.

- Top up water levels in ponds if necessary.
- Remove algae and duckweed.

THIN OUT OR CUT BACK pond and marginal plants which are growing more rapidly than you had expected, because at this time of year they will be putting on an immense amount of growth and could potentially swamp others. Oxygenators in particular are likely to be growing rapidly and if necessary simply pull out clumps of these and either compost them or give them to a pond-owning friend.

You may need to top up water levels. Temperatures are likely to be particularly high during this month and many ponds will lose a lot of water by evaporation and from the plants' transpiration. Ensure that all the plants are at the correct depth and wildlife still has easy access in and out of the pond.

Continue to clear out algae such as blanket weed and also duckweed on a regular basis (see page 73). It may still be worth using barley straw mats (see page 88) to keep that green 'pea soup' effect at bay.

An established pond with a good array of both marginal and deeper water plants looks stunning, but many of the plants will need thinning out eventually

FIXTURES AND FITTINGS

HOSE OFF garden chairs and tables at regular intervals, removing all traces of food or drink – even tiny amounts can encourage ants and wasps, both of which can be a real nuisance.

When choosing garden lighting consider including some candles or flares which incorporate citronella oils to keep mosquitoes at bay.

Before lighting a barbecue make sure that the heat it produces will not harm any nearby plants.

August

With temperatures likely to be high and rainfall low this is often deemed to be the holiday month, the time to put your feet up and recuperate for a week or two. Well, the great thing is that if an annual break means leaving the garden to its own devices, August is a relatively good month to do so. True, watering tends to be fairly time-consuming, and if there are crops to harvest you may well need to get someone to do both these jobs for you, but apart from that, growth often slows up somewhat, so sneaking off for a while should not be too much of a problem.

If this is a month when you have time to stay at home and enjoy your garden, August is usually great for this too, with plenty of colourful flowers and a good supply of home-grown crops too. A little bit of casual pottering around in the garden is pure pleasure, so it pays to keep up with deadheading, the odd bit of pest control, some routine weeding and of course mowing the lawn while surrounded by a good-looking garden and, with any luck, some sunshine.

GENERAL TASKS

WEEDS GROW VERY FAST at this time of year, particularly if the ground is watered periodically or there is some rain. As soon as conditions get drier many weeds also set seed particularly rapidly, so regular weeding is all the more important. Try to weed on really hot, dry days so that the weeds can be left to shrivel up and die on the soil surface.

It is also important to check plants regularly for pests and diseases, as many build up rapidly at this time of year. Some infections such as powdery mildews are much worse when the soil conditions are dry, so always check foliage for this. If the weather has been relatively damp, towards the end of the month you are also likely to see rust infections (see page 118) moving into many plants in all areas of the garden. Pick off or prune out severely affected leaves if possible, as this will help to keep disease levels relatively low next year. If time is very short, you can leave infected material on the plant until you have more time later on, but in doing this you could be making a rod for your own back.

If towards the end of summer your garden is less colourful than you had hoped, treat yourself to a few garden visits this month – you can enjoy a lovely snoop around someone else's plot and, provided you take a notebook, you can also borrow a few ideas for plants to add to your garden and particularly good plant combinations.

TREES, SHRUBS AND CLIMBERS

ESSENTIALS

If time is really short, try to fit these jobs in.

- Water as necessary, concentrating on newer plantings.
- Keep weeds down to minimise competition.
- Collect fallen diseased leaves from beneath trees, shrubs and climbers.
- Deadhead roses and lavenders.
- Prune rambler roses as soon as flowering is over.
- Finish summer pruning wisterias.

DURING DRY WEATHER water regularly and thoroughly, paying particular attention to any tree, shrub or climber that went in this spring or that has put on an unusually large amount of growth.

Continue to weed around the bases of garden plants. At this time of year moisture can be in short supply and it is essential that your garden plants use what is available, not weeds.

Collect up diseased leaves from beneath roses on a regular basis. Those infected with black spot, mildew or rust are likely to fall prematurely and you should remove these so as to decrease the likelihood of severe problems next year.

Clear up fallen leaves from beneath all trees, shrubs and climbers whenever you have the time. You can assume that leaves that have fallen in any quantity by now are likely to have something wrong with them and so bin or burn them to be on the safe side. If you have many trees and shrubs, consider investing in a garden vacuum, which is extremely efficient and will make the job far quicker. In smaller gardens, the tool you need is a spring-tined rake, which of course is also brilliant for removing moss and thatch from your lawn.

Continue to deadhead roses and other shrubs and climbers as soon as the flowers fade (see pages 93 and 94). The only exception are those which have particularly attractive seed heads which are part of the charm of the plant – such as many clematis with their lovely fluffy seed heads which are a really welcome sight in autumn and winter.

Trim or cut back hedges towards the end of the month – including conifer hedges not dealt with last month. With conifers, preferably get the job done towards the beginning of August. For deciduous plants this is probably the last cut you will need to make this year, but conifers often require a further trimming in October. For larger hedges a powered trimmer is a fantastic investment, as it will make a huge difference to the rate at which you can carry out the job. Hand shears are fine for smaller hedges, but always make sure that they are really sharp, or else the job will take far longer, prove to be particularly hard on you and leave ragged, untidy ends on the stems. Always try to follow the existing shape of the hedge, and make sure that the lower part of the hedge is wider than the top, as this makes it more weather resistant. It's much easier to get a good end result if you start by cutting back the sides of your hedge; and always start at the bottom and work your way up. Starting at the base is easier simply because all the shoots you cut off will fall to the ground, enabling you to see the shape that you have produced so far. Topiary also benefits from a final trim this month. Use special topiary clippers or shears, or a good, sharp pair of secateurs.

Trimming hedges can be hard work, so try to avoid the heat of the day, and ideally do the job on a relatively cool day

Give lavender plants a haircut using a pair of shears. Remove the old flower spikes and try also to take about 2.5cm (1in) of the leafy shoot tips as this will help to keep plants dense and bushy.

Prune rambling roses as soon as they have finished flowering. Prune back all side shoots that bore flowers this year, taking them back to one or two buds from the main stem. Cut back any old, damaged or diseased stems to ground level. Once you have done this it will be easier to tie in new and vigorous stems to the support system and you will find that the rose flowers all the better for having received this attention. If you find the whole business of tying stems in fiddly, there are numerous special clips and rings which have been developed especially to make this sort of task much easier and quicker, so see what is available at your local garden centre.

Make sure that you have finished all summer pruning of wisterias by the middle of this month (see page 93).

Feed any trees or shrubs in containers. Early August is the last date for this job; feed any later than this and you are likely to encourage soft growth, which will be damaged by frosts. Choose a high-potash liquid feed (such as a tomato fertiliser): this helps to toughen up or ripen woody stems, making them less prone to frost damage and, in some cases, more inclined to flower next year.

Check and replace or adjust tree ties and ties on climbers and trained wall shrubs before autumn winds arrive. Check for any signs of tightness after the summer's growth, chafing or deteriorating ties.

Sow and plant

- Propagate shrubs using semi-ripe cuttings at the beginning of this month (see page 94).

- Unless the weather is unusually cool and damp, avoid planting this month. In just a few weeks' time, autumn will be here and it is so much easier for plants to establish well then.

Pruning rambler roses

Prune out any dead, diseased or damaged growth, taking it back to a healthy outward-facing bud. Cut back the side shoots by about 15cm (6in) or 60 per cent, pruning back to a healthy outward-facing bud. Carefully tie in new shoots to the wire H-framework, making sure they are well spaced.

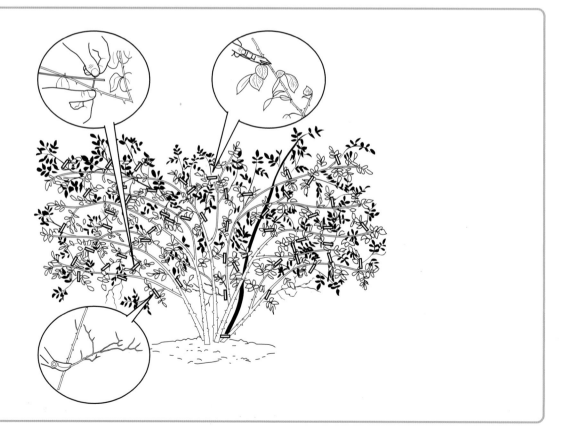

FLOWERS

ESSENTIALS

If time is really short, try to fit these jobs in.

- Weed regularly to minimise competition in beds and borders.
- Deadhead summer bedding plants, and feed those in containers with a high-potash fertiliser.
- Order bulbs from catalogues.

SORT OUT HERBACEOUS perennials that have become overgrown or floppy. In some years, especially if the weather has been warm and damp, you can be taken by surprise even by a plant that you thought you knew well: good growing conditions can result in excessive growth that causes plants to grow taller than you had expected and so develop a tendency to flop or collapse. This not only looks a mess but can also spoil adjacent plants or, if the plants are growing next to your lawn, cause the grass to die back. Take a sharp pair of secateurs to any overgrown plants or if necessary add to existing supports and stakes. If you feel tempted not to spend time doing this, remember that not only will it benefit the look of the border and the plants it contains right now, but in some cases you will also find that the plants put on a second flush of flowers later on.

Give haircuts, using shears, to any hardy geraniums that have just finished flowering (see page 95).

Continue to weed regularly in any gaps between herbaceous perennials. It is essential to remove them before they spoil the shape of your border plants or cause too much competition.

Regularly put by a few moments to pinch out faded flower heads on summer bedding plants in borders and containers. This really does make a world of difference, prolonging the flowering period and increasing the number of flowers you get to enjoy.

Confine to the compost heap any annuals that really have no chance of continuing to perform. From the middle or end of this month, there will be some of these: some plants have a flowering

Top ways to prolong shows from summer bedding

Keep plants well watered.

If the compost in a container dries out, stand the container in water for an hour or two.

Feed with a high-potash fertiliser at least every two weeks.

Remove faded flowers promptly.

Check for pests and diseases and treat problems promptly.

If an entire plant dies, remove it and replace it with something new.

Colchicums are a real delight, whether you choose single forms or one like this double 'Waterlily'

• **Send off for a few bulb catalogues,** if you have not already done so. The selection of bulbous plants that you can obtain from some of the more specialist nurseries is amazing and the prices are often very reasonable too. The great thing about shopping by post for this type of plant is that you should not be tempted to spend quite so much as you would in a garden centre and also you can fit in your 'catalogue shopping' in a few moments to spare when it is not possible to get on with any jobs in the garden.

• **Start buying spring–flowering bulbs.** If you have already got bulb catalogues, make sure you place your order promptly. If you have decided you prefer to shop at your local nursery or garden centre, you should find that spring-flowering bulbs are normally for sale from about the second or third week of this month, with an even wider range normally available by the end of August or early September.

• **Treat yourself to something really special and plant a few Madonna lily bulbs.** Choose a warm spot with well-drained soil in full sun. If the soil is in the slightest bit heavy, incorporate plenty of grit and plant the bulb on top of 2.5cm (1in) or so of grit.

• **Early in the month plant up a few colchicums** if you did not do so in July (see page 97). It is essential to get them into the ground now as they flower in the autumn.

period that naturally ends earlier than others, and in addition anything that has been subjected to drought or other stresses is likely to come to a premature end. It is best to admit this, clear the space and pop in something else that will provide colour well into autumn.

Continue to feed all bedding plants, particularly those in containers, using a high-potash liquid feed (see page 97).

If you are about to go on holiday, persuade (or if necessary bribe!) a friend or neighbour to keep an eye on your plants while you are away (see page 92). For the plants this could make the difference between thriving and not surviving, so it is essential, unless of course you have set up a drip or trickle irrigation system for your containers (see page 96).

THE LAWN

ESSENTIALS

If time is really short, try to fit these jobs in.

- Mow the lawn as necessary, keeping the cut quite high if the weather is dry.
- Keep relatively new lawns watered during dry weather.

MOW YOUR LAWN and any other grassy areas as necessary, according to the weather conditions, as for July (see page 98).

Unless the weather is extremely hot and dry, it may well be worth feeding the lawn. Make sure that you choose a suitable fertiliser, preferably one sold as an autumn lawn feed. If you apply this towards the end of August it should help to toughen up the grass for the winter ahead. Autumn lawn feeds contain a relatively high proportion of phosphate, which encourages good root growth. Do not use a spring fertiliser on the lawn, as the high nitrogen content in this may produce growth that is very soft and therefore prone to damage in winter. If you have a large lawn, it may well be worth hiring, buying or borrowing a wheeled lawn fertiliser spreader, which can be calibrated to apply granular fertilisers at precisely the right rate, making it a lot quicker and easier to perform this potentially boring task. Remember that most lawn feeds need to be watered in if rain does not follow, so try to time feeding so that at least this part of the job is done by nature.

Keep relatively newly laid or sown lawns adequately watered (see page 98).

Prepare the ground for new lawns, if you intend to lay or sow a new lawn this autumn (see page 29). Preparing the ground a little in advance will give you the chance to remove at least one batch of new weed seedlings before you sow or lay the turf.

A relatively new lawn, whether sown or created from turf, will need regular watering during drier weather

HERBS AND VEGETABLES

ESSENTIALS

If time is really short, try to fit these jobs in.

- Water crops during dry weather.
- Harvest crops regularly and promptly, so as to enjoy the biggest, tastiest and most tender meals possible.
- Hoe off weeds between rows regularly.
- Remove side shoots from tomatoes.

KEEP VEGETABLE CROPS adequately watered, especially those that are likely to bolt or run to seed if allowed to get too dry. Apply the water in the evening if at all possible, as this hugely reduces wastage. Top up mulches if necessary to aid soil moisture retention.

Continue to harvest crops regularly and frequently. It really is true that the more you pick the more you get when it comes to crops such as courgettes, marrows, beans and peas. Even if you are growing only a few plants it is still possible to have a miniature glut. If that is the case, rather than slowing up your picking rate, carry on and give the delicious produce to friends and family, or freeze it.

If you have grown onions or garlic, these crops should be ready to harvest this month if you did not lift them in July.

Hoe off weeds between vegetable plants regularly to prevent competition.

Continue to remove side shoots from tomatoes as soon as they appear (see page 70).

PROBLEM OF THE MONTH: BLOSSOM END ROT

If the base of the fruits of tomatoes or peppers turn black and leathery and sink in somewhat, they have got what is known as blossom end rot. Despite its name it is not actually a fungal rot but the result of a deficiency of calcium within the plants. Calcium is needed for cell wall structure and if there is not enough of it in the fruit, the cells at the blossom end collapse, causing blackening and flattening. Simply remove affected fruits (you can eat the top red bit if there is enough of it) and then keep the plants really well watered, ensuring that the compost is good and moist at all times. If the compost is dry, it prevents the calcium being taken up by the plant and so blossom end rot is much more likely. Make a note in your diary to buy bigger containers for your tomatoes next year, as larger compost volume makes drying out less of a problem. Instead of using growing bags for tomatoes or peppers, consider growing them in large tubs or using a full-size bag of compost. Also consider installing a trickle or drip irrigation system into pots and bags of these blossom end rot prone plants.

Regularly check tomato plants and remove any leaves that are showing signs of grey mould. This fuzzy grey fungal growth is particularly likely to appear in plants grown in greenhouses, porches or under other forms of protection, where the air is inclined to be stagnant. If you see this fungus developing on the stem, it is best to cut out the whole area in order to prevent it from spreading.

Remove a few leaves from tomatoes growing in greenhouses, conservatories or porches in order to let more light through to the developing fruits.

As soon as the 'silks' on sweet corn start to turn brown, it means that that particular cob is ready to be harvested. Try to pick the cobs as close as possible to eating time because as soon as the cob is off the plant the sugars start to turn to starch, causing a loss in sweetness.

Sow and plant

- Continue to make late sowings of salad leaves and other salad ingredients (see page 100).

FRUIT

ESSENTIALS

If time is really short, try to fit these jobs in.

- Cut back any summer-fruiting raspberries not dealt with already.
- Finish pruning cordon apples and pears.
- Plant new strawberry plants in open ground or in containers.

IT IS TIME TO START picking earlier-cropping apples. Ensure that the fruit really is ready for picking by gently cupping one in your hand and giving it a subtle twist. If the fruit is ripe it will easily come away from the tree.

Look out for brown rot disease on apples, pears and plums. This can be seen as brownish rotting covered with numerous raised creamy, white pustules. Infection occurs via damage on the fruit surface, and you should remove and dispose of infected fruits promptly.

Prune out any summer-fruiting raspberries that were not dealt with last month (see page 101).

Summer prune espalier apple and pear trees. Simply cut back all the new long shoots produced over the summer, pruning back to about three buds from the branch from which they originate. Then prune back the growth on the side shoots that you pruned last year. By now these will have produced side shoots themselves and these need to be taken back to about 2.5cm (1in).

Pruning cordon apple and pear trees, taking back all the shoots that have grown from the main stem to about 7.5cm (3in). Shoots that were pruned in this way last year will now have produced side shoots themselves and these need to be cut back to about 2.5cm (1in).

- Plant up a strawberry pot. There are numerous attractive terracotta strawberry pots available and these certainly look delightful when the plants are in flower or fruiting. However, if you want something much easier to maintain and less inclined to dry out, simply buy yourself a large container, put some crocks in the bottom and fill it with a mixture of John Innes No. 2 and a multi-purpose loam-free compost. You could create a very good-looking yet fairly low-maintenance strawberry planter by using three terracotta pots – one large, one medium and one small. Ideally choose shallow or half pots and fill each with compost; then stack them on top of each other, with the largest at the base, and plant your strawberries in the ring of compost in the large and medium pot and in the whole surface of the small pot. I find that the larger volume of compost makes it much easier to keep the plants adequately watered.

A home-made strawberry 'tower' like this is much easier to maintain than a traditional strawberry pot

PONDS AND WATER FEATURES

ESSENTIALS

If time is really short, try to fit these jobs in.

- Top up water levels in ponds and water features.
- Pick or cut off deteriorating pond and marginal plant leaves.

TOP UP WATER LEVELS IN PONDS (see page 103) and make sure that all water features have proper water levels.

When watering plants in your garden, also water your pond and any water features. This type of watering is not really to increase water levels but to introduce some oxygen into the water, so making it a better environment for plants and wildlife and helping to decrease problems with algae.

Carefully remove algae and duckweed from the pond before it starts to build up (see page 73).

Cut off any yellowed and deteriorating leaves that develop on pond and marginal plants. Leaves are especially likely to start to yellow towards the end of the month and if you allow these to flop into the water and deteriorate as they rot down they will produce methane and other gases which can prove toxic to fish and other pond wildlife over the winter months. In addition, deteriorating leaves tend to encourage algal growth and that is the last thing you want. You will find that once tidied up the pond looks so much neater.

Hot summer weather may cause a lot of water to be lost from the pond by evaporation, so water levels may need to be topped up

September

This late summer–early autumn weather is great,
but also variable, and it brings with it a host of things
that you should try to get done in your garden.
Many view September as one of the best months
for planting, and if you grow fruit or vegetables
September will also provide you with plenty of
reminders about why growing-your-own is so good.

So combine a bit of hard work with some serious
munching of fruit or home-grown vegetables and
you'll find that this month has the potential to be
one of your favourite months in the garden.

GENERAL TASKS

WARM AND OFTEN MOIST WEATHER provides perfect conditions for many pests and pathogens, so the potential for problems this month is bigger than normal, but the good thing is that on the whole, damage that occurs this late in the year has little if any effect on a plant's long-term health and performance. It makes a lot of sense to check regularly for pests and diseases and to remove or treat obvious problems; but with many, such as powdery mildews, cutting off the worst-affected areas may suffice, and you can often get away with turning a blind eye to problems on the foliage now – simply have a very thorough clean-up when you have the time in the next month or so.

It may be hard work, but it is well worth digging in bulky organic matter and maybe even some grit, especially if you have a heavy clay soil, where digging in grit will improve drainage. This helps to improve the soil texture and increase aeration, and the manure or compost will also act as some good, natural slow-release fertiliser. Remember that all the effort you put in now will mean better results from your garden, and if you do it before the soil gets too wet, it will be a lot easier on your muscles. Conditioning the soil in this way is important preparation for any planting you may be doing.

TREES, SHRUBS AND CLIMBERS

ESSENTIALS
If time is really short, try to fit these jobs in.

- Move any trees and shrubs that are not suited to their present position.
- Prune climbing roses as soon as they finish flowering.
- Get planting – trees, shrubs and climbers.

MOVE TREES and shrubs if necessary. This is a good time to move small deciduous trees and shrubs that are in the wrong place – the longer the plant has been in the ground the greater the risk there is in moving it, but provided the soil is already quite moist and you take a really good-sized root ball, you are in with a chance this month. Prepare the new planting hole and then dig up the plant, taking as large a root ball as you can safely manage. Persuade a friend to help if possible and remember that it may be easier to move a large plant if you place it directly into a wheelbarrow or on to a tough groundsheet. It is essential not to allow the roots to dry out at all, so wrap the root ball in some damp hessian or old sacks, or cover it with polythene. Ease the plant into the new planting hole, checking that it will be planted at the same depth

PROBLEM OF THE MONTH: RUST FUNGI

Rust fungi thrive and spread quickly and easily in the relatively mild and yet moist weather conditions so often found this month. Typical symptoms include orange or dark brown spores grouped in circles, spots or within pustules, causing leaf yellowing and possible premature leaf drop. On some non-edible plants you can spray with a suitable fungicide, but where this is not possible, or if you would simply prefer to reduce spraying, try to minimise spread by collecting up or picking off infected areas promptly, improving air circulation and avoiding wetting the foliage.

as before, and then pull the sheet or sacking away from beneath it. Backfill the hole with soil, firming it as you go, and water well to ensure that the soil settles around the roots. A tree that is quite tall may, if the site is windy, need a sloping stake for the first couple of years. Evergreens are best moved in spring (see page 35).

Prune climbing roses that have finished flowering. Some may still be looking good, in which case you can delay this task until October. Using sharp secateurs, prune out dead, diseased, damaged and dying stems. Tie in new healthy-looking stems to the support, ensuring that there is enough room for some, but not excessive, movement. Prune old stems right back to ground level. Prune back side shoots on the branches of the existing main body of the rose to about three buds.

Sow and plant

• As soon as the weather starts to cool, get planting container-grown trees, shrubs and climbers. If you do it early on they will have even longer to start to get themselves established before the onset of the warmer, drier weather in the spring.

FLOWERS

REGULARLY DEADHEAD faded flowers on plants in containers and borders – there may not be much flowering potential left, but you might as well do anything you can to squeeze that little bit more out if possible. Muggy weather may also encourage infections, which often start on dead or dying plant material, so that is another good reason to get snipping or pinching.

Lift and divide clumps of established and overcrowded herbaceous perennials that have finished putting on their main display for the year. If left to its own devices, an overcrowded plant will start to look quite miserable and its flowering potential will decline rapidly. It usually becomes quite obvious when it is time to divide a plant, as the centre of the clump starts to deteriorate and become rather thin, and the plant generally stops performing as well as it did in the past. Using a garden or border fork, carefully lift the entire clump and place it on a sheet of heavy-duty polythene on your terrace or patio or on some vacant ground, then insert two forks back to back in the centre of the clump and ease them apart. The plant should naturally start to divide up into suitable sections for replanting; you should end up with several smaller but vigorous new plants. Always get rid of any sickly or miserable-looking pieces. Most of these will be towards the centre of the clump, as the newer more vigorous growth is generally towards the outside. For clumps of smaller herbaceous perennials use two hand forks back to back or just pull the clumps apart with your hands. For some really tough plants you may need a stout-bladed knife; or, in extreme situations, you may need to cut it up using a sharp spade. When you replant the new sections, improve the soil around the roots so as to set each off to a fresh start.

Make sure that autumn-flowering herbaceous plants, such as Japanese anemones, sedums and asters, or Michaelmas daisies have adequate supports. Weather can be variable this month and if the plants get quite tall, and worse still if there is then some fairly heavy rain or gusty wind, the whole clump can flop. Placing a few canes strategically or readjusting existing supports may be all you need to do.

Lift and divide crocosmias and montbretias. These provide a fantastic show of really striking flower spikes in late summer and early autumn, but this display will soon decline if the clumps become congested and overcrowded. Once the plants have finished flowering and the leaves are starting to yellow, use a garden fork to lift the entire clump and then divide it up. With very old clumps this can be an incredibly difficult job as the corms and their roots become quite tightly knit. You can save a lot of time and energy if you first squirt the base of the clump firmly with a strong jet of water from the garden hose. Then pull the clump apart, using your hands or a knife, and replant all the healthy-looking clumps 12–15cm (5–6in) apart.

To keep tender perennial plants for next year, lift them by the middle of this month and keep them in a frost-free place or else they will be killed off as soon as the temperatures start to drop. Such plants include pelargoniums, osteospermums and argyranthemums. Cut back each plant slightly to remove deteriorating flowers and leaves and then pot it into a container of fresh compost. If you do not have a frost-free greenhouse or cold frame, a shed or unheated garage or even a utility room will do. The plants need to be kept only just moist; if anything you should err on the side of less water rather than more, as if they are the slightest bit too damp they may start to deteriorate. There is certainly a feel-good factor involved in keeping plants such as these from year to year, but if space and time are short, you can simply be hard-hearted and pop them on the compost heap or allow them to take their chances outside, perhaps with a bit of protection. It is unlikely that they will survive and if they do not you will need to buy new plants again next year.

Feed containers that include herbaceous perennials with sulphate of potash or rock potash. This will toughen up the plants slightly and increase their chances of winter survival. Do not apply any other feeds to these containers as they encourage soft growth, which will make the plants more prone to damage by frosts.

Top biennials to plant out in September

Anchusa

Canterbury bells (*Campanula*)

Forget-me-nots (*Myosotis*)

Foxgloves (*Digitalis*)

Iceland poppies (*Papaver nudicaule*)

Sweet William (*Dianthus barbutus*)

Wallflowers (*Erysimum*)

Winter-flowering daisies – pompom bellis (*Bellis perennis*)

Feed, water and deadhead regularly summer bedding in pots, baskets and window boxes. In most areas this will put on a good display at least until the middle of September and sometimes later, and by doing a little bit of maintenance like this, you will keep the display going for as long as possible.

Remove any containers of summer bedding which have definitely passed their best. Don't be tempted to re-use the compost, as doing this hugely increases the chances of soil-borne pests and diseases becoming a problem; vine weevil in particular often thrives in gardens where a lot of container compost is re-used repeatedly. Instead, clear out the container properly, dry it off and then put it in a shed or garage for the winter. Better still, once you've cleaned it up, re-use the container for a display of autumn, winter or spring colour and interest.

Sow and plant

• Think ahead and introduce some spring colour now by planting some spring-flowering biennials

(see box). Many of these will be available in garden centres now and some, such as wallflowers, are extremely good value if bought bare root or from a pick-your-own outlet. Dig or fork over the soil and incorporate bulky organic matter, then plant out the biennials, ensuring that each is at the correct level, with only the roots below the soil. Occasionally bare-root plants may have rather confusing soil levels on them because they have been heeled in: it is essential that they do not go in too deep. Once the plants are in the ground, firm the soil and then water them in to settle the soil around the roots.

• A quick trip to any good garden centre or nursery at this time of year will reveal a whole host of herbaceous perennials which are just itching to be planted. The soil should now still be fairly warm as a result of summer sunshine and yet recent rain will have made it fairly moist. If it is still quite dry, delay planting until towards the end of this month or even into October.

The great thing about getting these plants into the ground now is that you can also save yourself a considerable amount of money by buying the

Planting perennials

1 Hold the pot in one hand and squeeze it firmly while supporting the topgrowth in the other hand. Now loosened, the plant should come out of the pot more easily.

2 Holding the rootball in one hand carefully tease out the roots with the other.

3 Most herbaceous perennials need to be planted so that the top of the compost is level with the soil surface.

plants when they are relatively small and inexpensive and you'll find that they soon catch up with larger and pricier specimens. When choosing plants always check that the things you fall for are really suitable for the site you have in mind. Pay particular attention to the section of the label that states the type of conditions the plant needs – there really is little point in growing a plant requiring full sun in fairly dense shade as it will bear little resemblance to the plant you had hoped for and is unlikely to produce any worthy flowers. The ultimate height and spread should help you consider where to position the plant. It seems a shame to plant a delicate new herbaceous perennial immediately behind something that has

got the potential to be much taller or broader. Similarly, particularly when you buy a small plant, it may seem unbelievable that it can get as big as the label states, but this information is pretty reliable and so do ensure that when you plant up your border, you leave adequate space between plants. If you don't, the initial effect may look more impressive, but within a year or at most two, the whole bed will become overcrowded, and the plants will be cramped and not performing as they should. If you find the bare space between the plants upsetting in these early stages, the best thing to do is to pop in some seasonal bedding to brighten things up until the other herbaceous perennials broaden out.

• This is the best month for planting most spring-flowering bulbs (with the exception of tulips, which should ideally be planted in November to minimise the risk of their succumbing to diseases particular to tulips). Send off for the bulbs or pay a visit to your favourite local garden centre. Bulbs are tremendous value as in most cases once they are planted, provided you give them a little bit of maintenance, they last and perform well for years and years. Many, such as narcissus or daffodils, are also unbelievably inexpensive when you consider the show that they will give you. Before going shopping, decide where you think you

Top things to look out for when buying a plant

Healthy foliage that is a good green colour (or whatever the colour is meant to be for the variety you have chosen).

No signs of pests or diseases.

A root system that is not overcrowded, but just fills the pot.

A compost surface that is free from weeds, liverworts and mosses.

Plenty of strong healthy growth or shoots.

Top spring flowering bulbs for planting this month

Alliums

Anemone blanda

Camassia

Chionodoxa

Crocus

Daffodils – miniature

Daffodils– full size

Dwarf iris

Muscari

Scillas

would like to see some spring colour – there is a bulb to suit almost any position in the garden and don't forget that most look lovely in pots or other containers too. Each type of bulb needs to be planted at a different depth, so check the packet for instructions. If you want to do quite a bit of planting, and especially if you want some bulbs to naturalise in grass, it is worth buying yourself a bulb planting tool. This is an inexpensive bit of kit and certainly makes the job a lot easier. You can get hand planters or, for a fair amount more money, tools that can be driven into the ground using your foot – these really are fantastically back-saving and useful.

Most bulbs look best in informal clumps or drifts. Provided you plant them at approximately the right spacing (this will be stated clearly on the pack) one of the best ways to achieve a really natural look is to gently throw a handful of bulbs on the soil surface and then plant them where they land, just taking care to separate out any that have landed too close to each other. Some people react to bulbs and can end up with a skin irritation: if you fear this might be the case with

you, wear either gardening gloves or disposable plastic gloves. If the soil is dry, water the bulbs in well and if your soil is extremely heavy it may be worth incorporating some good sharp grit in the area as well when planting. If mice or squirrels tend to steal bulbs from your garden, make a cage of narrow-mesh chicken wire and placing it over the area where you have just planted the bulbs. Once they have rooted well, and certainly once they have started to produce top growth, it is unlikely that they will be dug up, so the rather ugly chicken wire does not have to stay there too long.

In small gardens, consider planting your favourite bulbs in open-sided boxes or crates – pond baskets work perfectly. Much as I love spring-flowering bulbs, there is no escaping the fact that the deteriorating foliage is not a particularly attractive sight, but if planted this way once the bulbs have finished flowering, and as soon as they start to die back, you can carefully lift the box or basket out of the soil and allow their foliage to die down as it needs to in an out-of-the-way spot. You can then plant something pretty in their place, and re-plunge the basket in the border next autumn.

• Spring-flowering bulbs look great in grass, particularly beneath a tree or large shrub. A few bulbs forming a drift look stunning. Planting bulbs in an existing area of grass is called naturalising them as, once they have been planted, you basically let them get on with it, only occasionally feeding them. To naturalise bulbs, remember that you should try to choose an area of grass that can be left to get a bit long and unkempt, as you will not be able to cut the grass until the leaves of the bulbs have started to die down naturally. (If you cut them down too early the bulbs may not have enough energy in them to produce a good show of flowers the following year.) You can use a bulb planter or narrow sharp trowel to create individual planting holes for bulbs in grass. Alternatively, if you want to plant a large number of smaller bulbs, it is far easier to carefully cut an H-shape in the grass, using the blade of a sharp spade, and then gently peel back the two oblongs of turf. Loosen up the soil beneath, plant small bulbs such as crocus and then replace the flaps of turf, firming them down gently and giving them a good soaking to ensure that the turf roots back properly.

Top bulbs for naturalising in grass	
Allium moly	*Galanthus nivalis*
Anemone blanda	*Leucojum aestivum*
Chionodoxa	*Leucojum vernum*
Colchicum autumnale	Narcissus
Colchicum speciosum	– large and dwarf forms
Crocus	*Scilla bifolia*
Erythronium dens-canis	*Tulipa sprengerii*
Fritillaria meleagris	

THE LAWN

ESSENTIALS

If time is really short, try to fit these jobs in.

- Re-seed bare patches.
- Get to grips with autumn lawn care – scarifying, aerating and feeding.
- Create new lawn from grass seed or turf.

REMOVE BROAD-LEAVED WEEDS from the lawn, using a sharp trowel, daisy grubber or suitable lawn weedkiller (see page 69).

Sow grass seed on bare patches. These develop on lawns after you have removed quite a bit of weed growth or perhaps as a result of wear and tear over the summer months. Using a rake, roughen up the earth and then simply sprinkle a suitable grass seed mixture on to the soil and re-rake it to incorporate the seed. If necessary, add a small amount of sieved garden soil or compost. Then gently press down over the re-seeded area with the back of the rake. Provided the grass seed is kept adequately watered at all times, it should germinate well at this time of year and the bare area will soon be covered. However, if you want to speed things up, and ensure that your grass seed does not make an easy meal for local birds, peg down a piece of clear polythene over the re-seeded patch to create a miniature cloche. As soon as the tiny grass shoots start to appear, you must remove the polythene. Or protect from birds with a few twiggy sticks until the grass is growing away well.

Don't ignore mowing completely. Weather conditions can be variable this month, but you should need to spend far less time mowing the lawn, which comes as a great relief to most of us. However, although the grass can be allowed to get slightly longer in preparation for winter, it must not get out of control.

Try to do some basic autumn lawn care. September is one of the main months for this. In most areas and in most seasons the bulk of the work needs to be done towards the end of the month or into early October. The amount of lawn maintenance you do depends on the quality of lawn you aspire to and also the amount of time you have to spare. There is, however, no doubt that every half-hour of time put in now will make a significant difference to the lawn's appearance next year.

Use a spring-tined rake to remove the 'thatch' that gathers around the base of each grass plant. Thatch is largely composed of dead grass, dead moss and other organic debris and if it is allowed to accumulate it can prevent adequate air getting down to the roots of the grass and also interfere with drainage; this will result in more weed and moss problems and a generally less healthy lawn, which will be prone to all sorts of problems. Moss must be killed before you attempt to rake it out, so if necessary use a moss killer a couple of weeks before scarifying. On a small lawn all you have to do is aggressively rake the surface with the spring-tined rake, but if you have a large lawn or if time is short it is worth hiring, buying or borrowing a lawnmower attachment or a mechanical scarifier. Whichever method you use, the lawn will look an awful lot worse when you have finished, as a good deal of the greenness and density will have been taken away, often revealing a scarily obvious amount of bare soil. Don't panic: this is always the case. That extra oxygen and moisture the grasses can now receive will work wonders. If you have a larger lawn, invest in, borrow or hire an electric scarifier, which will make the job much quicker and much easier.

Alleviate compaction. Lawns easily become compacted, particularly on heavy soil, after a summer of heavy use and in areas where the grass has taken a great pounding. Compacted soil around the grass leads to poor aeration of the roots and again a generally unhealthy and more disease-prone lawn. Improving aeration is, therefore, an important part of autumn lawn care. On small lawns you can do this quite well by just driving a garden fork into the soil to a depth of about 15cm (6in) and at about 15cm (6in) intervals across any compacted area, and you will see a noticeable difference. However, if you have a larger lawn or simply need to save time, you may be able to hire, borrow or buy a mechanical aerator. Most of these are known as hollow-tine aerators and remove cores or plugs of soil, creating drainage channels. If you then brush a sandy topsoil mixture or top dressing across the lawn surface these drainage channels remain open for longer, and you should not need to repeat the process more than once every few years.

Feed your lawn with a specially formulated autumn lawn feed if you did not do so last month (see page 111).

Sow and plant

• September or early October are generally considered the best months for creating a new lawn, either with turf or seed, but obviously the precise timing should depend on local weather conditions for that year. If you decide not to create a lawn now, you could do it in March instead. Whether you have decided to turf or grow grass from seed, good preparation (see page 29) greatly increases your chances of achieving a good-looking lawn and will also help to encourage it to establish quickly and easily – so making your initial aftercare a lot easier too. To lay turf, follow the instructions on page 41.

• If sowing lawn seed, as with turf it is essential that you plan your lawn-seeding operation at a time when you know you will be there to keep the seed adequately watered at all times, as it is obviously much more susceptible to drought damage when the seeds are germinating and when the seedlings grasses are young. To sow seed, first treat the area as described on page 41. Make sure that you have chosen a suitable grass seed mixture (see page 41) and then sprinkle the seed over the surface at the rate suggested on the pack. This is usually given as grams per square metre, which means very little unless you have done an awful lot of grass seed sowing! It is well worthwhile marking out a plot which measures exactly one square metre, and then, using kitchen scales, carefully measuring out the suggested amount of grass seed and sprinkling this evenly over the square metre area to give yourself a good idea of what the rate of sowing should look like. Some fertiliser spreaders are calibrated for use with grass seed and these are especially useful if time is short or you have a considerable area to cover. Once all the seed is in place, rake over the surface again to bury the grass seed and then, unless good rain is forecast, use a sprinkler to gently but evenly water the seed in. If birds are likely to be a problem (they may well steal the grass seed), you will need to put out some bird-scaring devices.

HERBS AND VEGETABLES

LIFT MAINCROP potatoes. Choose a fairly dry day so that you can leave the tubers on the soil surface for an hour or two to allow the skin to dry off thoroughly. Store only undamaged potatoes in a cool, but frost-free place in complete darkness. Store them in paper or hessian sacks, not in plastic or polythene, as this is likely to result in rotting.

Sow and plant

• If you fancy some home-grown onions, autumn is the best time to grow onions from onion sets. This is an amazingly simple operation: you just buy tiny onion bulbs which you plant about 7.5cm (3in) apart, covering them with just enough soil so that the tip of the miniature onion is protruding. It is worthwhile covering the crop with netting or fleece until the sets have rooted and the danger of bird damage is over. The miniature onions will then sit in the soil and increase in size until they are ready to harvest towards the end of next summer.

• Buy yourself a bulb or two of garlic from a garden centre or from a mail-order supplier, separate each bulb into cloves and then get planting in a good sunny site. (Do not risk economizing by using garlic from your greengrocer or supermarket, because though this may taste and look good, it is much more likely to be harbouring a virus infection and so would produce an inferior crop.) Place the cloves 7.5–10cm (3–4 in) apart and making sure that the tip of each clove is just covered by soil.

FRUIT

CUT BACK the last of the canes on summer-fruiting raspberries, if you have not already done so (see page 101).

September is one of the best months for enjoying crops of freshly picked apples and pears, although precise picking dates will vary with variety (see page 113).

Autumn-fruiting raspberries should also be producing heavy crops at this time of year and there is really nothing else to do other than to pick them regularly – you often need to do this once a day during sunny weather – and enjoy eating the fruits of your labours. Remember that the fruits can also be very successfully frozen for use later.

Erect taut netting or scaring devices around fruit trees if you anticipate having problems with birds.

To avoid winter moth problems on next year's crop of apples, fix grease bands around the trunks of trees. Fit these (they are available from all good garden centres and many mail-order suppliers) precisely according to the instructions and you will prevent winter moths from climbing up the trunk and so hugely reduce or completely avoid the damage that they can cause.

This month and over the next few months, prune blackcurrants if necessary (see page 18). To make the job a lot easier and more straightforward, wait until the leaves are starting to fall naturally.

Sow and plant

- This is a perfect month to plant container-grown fruit trees and bushes as the soil should still be fairly warm and moist. When choosing fruit trees remember that you may need a suitable pollinator growing close by (see pages 19 and 30).

- If you want some strawberries for next year and have not yet done so, make sure you plant them before the middle of this month, so as to give them a chance to produce useful amount of roots for establishment this autumn (see page 114).

PONDS AND WATER FEATURES

ESSENTIALS

If time is really short, try to fit these jobs in.

- Net ponds to keep autumn leaves out.
- Lift and divide overcrowded or congested pond plants.
- Cut off deteriorating foliage on pond plants and compost it.

STRETCH SOME GARDEN NETTING over the surface of your pond or water feature. If the pond is of a considerable size it helps to put a double layer of netting over the surface, with the lower layer held firmly in position by a series of bricks around the edge of the pond. Netting the pond in this way early in September ensures that leaves from nearby trees and shrubs do not fall into the water. If the pond becomes clogged with leaves not only is it a time-consuming job to clear it out but also any leaves that remain in it will produce potentially damaging gases as they break down. If these gases escape through the surface of the pond, they are of little consequence, but if the pond surface starts to ice over during the winter months the gases can do a lot of damage to pond inhabitants. The advantage of a double layer of netting is that when you lift the netting to empty the leaves off from time to time, it is much easier to get it in place over a large pond if there is already a supporting net over the entire surface.

Carefully lift any over-vigorous or congested plants from your pond and thin out, divide or cut back as appropriate (see page 58). This is not a job that you need to do every year, but something which should be tackled if it looks as if the plants could soon start to take over. If possible, lift the plant a couple of days before you divide it and stand it close to the edge of the pond so that any moisture-requiring creatures that were hiding among the foliage or even the roots can nip back out and into the water.

Continue to cut deteriorating or yellow leaves on pond plants and marginals (see page 115).

Double-netting a pond

A piece of wire mesh or wide-mesh wire netting, topped with a piece of lighter-weight netting and positioned over a pond before leaves start to fall makes keeping leaves out much easier – just lift the top mesh, empty the leaves and replace.

FIXTURES AND FITTINGS

Construct

• Make a leaf mould bin in an out-of-the-way spot in the garden. Drive four strong posts into the ground to create the corners. Then use a hammer and 'U' staples to attach galvanised chicken wire right the way around. Now you have a near-instant container into which you can pile fallen deciduous leaves and allow them to break down to create leaf mould, a fantastic material to dig in to improve soil texture or to use as a mulch, and a great use for all those leaves.

• Buy yourself a compost bin if you do not already have one, or, if you are DIY-capable, make one. The most useful systems have two or more berths so that you can be filling one side while the other is reaching maturity or being emptied. Position the bin somewhere where it cannot be considered an eyesore and get filling it so that you will soon be able to reap all the rewards of home-made compost for planting and mulching and general soil improving.

A leaf mould-bin is quick and easy to make and means you can turn old leaves into leafmould, a great soil improver

October

Autumn has definitely arrived and you will notice a distinct change in temperature and light levels. But any feeling of sadness that you may have that summer has finally gone now can surely be banished by looking at the wonderful array of autumn fruits of all types and the extraordinarily beautiful colours of the changing foliage. It's a great time to work in the garden as temperatures are obviously considerably cooler, but at the same time it is still very good weather for planting.

Shorter day lengths will, however, mean that if you go out to work you will have to do most of your gardening in a snatched few minutes on your return home or at the weekends – or, if you are feeling really in the gardening mood, in the odd day taken off work!

GENERAL TASKS

OCTOBER IS A FANTASTIC MONTH for planting, as even if September was a little dry, the soil is almost invariably moist by now and yet is unlikely to have taken on too much of a chill. It is also a great time to enjoy many of the edible crops you may have grown, and to stand back and take a look at the garden and decide if there are any major changes you want to make. If you have it in mind to plant anything new, now is the time to do it – so get planning and planting!

It is likely that every part of your garden will be being covered with a carpet of autumn leaves at some stage this month, so leaf raking (and then turning it into leaf mould) is a task that will keep recurring. If there are a number of tall trees close to your garden, it may seem an unending one, but some of the time you spend doing it may be compensated for by the fact that there are far fewer pests and diseases of importance around at this time of year, so that's one problem you don't have to worry about. If fallen leaves really do seem to be taking up a disproportionate amount of time, consider investing in a garden vacuum cleaner or leaf sucker, which will allow you to safely clear leaves in most parts of the garden, without any risk to nearby plants. The leaves are a wonderful resource and it is certainly essential that you do something useful with it – and what better than turn it into leaf mould? Making your own leaf mould cage is simple and inexpensive (see page 129).

With a little planning flower borders can still be packed with colour at this time of year – if in doubt seek inspiration from other people's efforts!

TREES, SHRUBS AND CLIMBERS

ESSENTIALS
If time is really short, try to fit these jobs in.

- Rake up fallen leaves regularly, especially those that appear to be diseased.
- Last chance to prune climbing roses.
- Prune conifer hedges.
- Plant container-grown trees, shrubs and climbers.

RAKE OR COLLECT UP fallen diseased leaves from beneath trees, shrubs and climbers. With many diseases this is one of the main ways to break their life cycle and to decrease the problems they cause next year. Many diseases that attack at this time of year are not of great significance. However, with some plants, such as roses, it is well worthwhile collecting up and disposing of any leaves that look in the slightest bit suspicious, as these plants can often become plagued by disease.

If you are planning to plant any bare-root trees, shrubs or hedging plants from next month onwards, it is a really good idea to prepare the soil this month, if you have the time. Dig or fork the area over thoroughly and incorporate some good bulky organic matter. As soon as any weeds appear, hoe them off. If you do this several times, you will find that you have made considerable inroads into the existing weed population.

Give any climbing roses that were not dealt with last month your urgent attention now (see page 119) and at the same time take the opportunity to clear up any fallen leaves beneath the plants.

Sow and plant

• This is a great month to plant container-grown trees, shrubs, climbers and hedging. For planting, see page 36. If you are after a hedge and want to cut back on time needed for planting, and on costs, consider planting a bare-root hedge instead of container-grown plants (see page 151).

1 Fork over the sides and base of a good-sized planting hole then incorporate some planting compost mixed with garden soil.

2 Gently but firmly tease out the roots, especially those towards the outer edge of the root ball. Cut out any which are dead or badly damaged.

3 Plant so that just the roots are below ground and the soil is well clear of the stems, water well and apply a mulch.

FLOWERS

ESSENTIALS
If time is really short, try to fit these jobs in.

- **Lift and divide congested clumps of herbaceous perennials.**
- **Clear fallen leaves from around herbaceous plants.**
- **Finish planting spring-flowering bulbs (except tulips).**
- **Plant some new herbaceous perennials to bring colour to beds and borders in the autumn months.**

LIFT THE LAST of your non-hardy or tender perennials (if you did not do so in September).

Cut or pick off any semi-evergreen leaves with powdery mildew. Some herbaceous perennials such as pulmonarias or lungworts tend to be semi-evergreen and their leaves often become quite extensively covered with powdery mildew in late summer and autumn. Removing the worst affected leaves will minimise disease spread and keep the plants looking as good as possible over the winter months. As you do this, take a few minutes to search beneath the lower leaves on your herbaceous plants and remove slugs and snails.

Overgrown or congested clumps of very well-established herbaceous perennials can be divided now. If soil conditions happen to be extremely wet or extremely dry, this job is best left until either next month or until early spring (see page 119).

Try to clear fallen leaves from flowerbeds on a regular basis, particularly if conditions are wet. Flowerbeds anywhere near sizeable deciduous trees or shrubs can become swamped by fallen autumn leaves. At first this may look pretty, as the leaves can form an attractive carpet, but you need to

Sow and plant

• Try to plant all spring-flowering bulbs by this month (with the exception of tulips) (see page 122). Planting these in the autumn allows the roots to get established. If you do not manage this, however, you should certainly not discard the bulbs, as if you plant them later they are unlikely to fail completely – you may simply get a rather delayed or slightly inferior show of flowers come the spring.

• Bring some beautiful blooms and fantastic perfume to your borders or terrace by planting some lilies (see page 122). Pots of lilies look and smell wonderful on a terrace or patio.

• Take a good look at flowerbeds and borders and if there is little of interest consider adding a few new plants (see page 121), either now or in the

With a little planning flower borders can still be packed with colour at this time of year – if in doubt seek inspiration from other people's efforts!

remove them as they tend to smother the less vigorous plants on which they fall and often moisture levels beneath them get quite high, causing the plants to deteriorate. If time is short, simply brush or rake the leaves off the plants and leave them on any bare soil in between. Doing this will certainly help to improve conditions around the plants, but do bear in mind that it may be a short-term solution, as the next gust of wind may well blow the leaves back on to the plants!

spring. There are plenty of plants that will provide really good colour from late summer, say August, right through until the autumn, and provided they are given a suitable position they will make a huge difference to the look of your garden at this time of year.

Top late summer/autumn colour plants

Amelanchier lamarckii

Chrysanthemum

Heuchera (foliage)

Cimicifuga simplex

Colchicum

Cotinus

Crocosmia 'Lucifer'

Echinacea

Euonymus alatus

Helenium

Ice plants (*Sedum*) including *S.* 'Autumn Joy' and 'Brilliant'

Japanese anemone (*Anemone* × *hybrida*)

Michaelmas daisy and related asters

Nerine bowdenii

Prunus – many kinds

Rudbeckia fulgida

Schizostylis coccinea

Tiarella (foliage)

Vitis coignetiae

Add colour to beds, borders and containers by adding a good selection of spring flowering bulbs now

THE LAWN

ESSENTIALS

If time is really short, try to fit these jobs in.

- Keep on with autumn lawn care.
- Mow the lawn if necessary.
- Create new lawns if the weather is still suitable.

CONTINUE WITH autumn lawn care (see page 125). If weather conditions were very wet or extremely dry last month, get on with this job now before conditions change yet again.

Cut new lawns if necessary, but take great care not to do this unless the new lawn is adequately well established (see page 69). Whatever you do, never cut a new lawn too low, as you can do some serious damage. At this time of year I would suggest cutting to 3–3.5cm (1½ to 1¾ in).

Mow an established lawn, if the surface is not too wet and it is still growing, keeping the blades fairly high.

Sow and plant

- Continue to lay turf (see page 41) and sow grass seed (see page 125) to create new lawns, provided the weather seems all right. If it has either become too cold or too wet, you should wait until the spring.

HERBS AND VEGETABLES

- Clear up any vegetable plants that have ceased being productive, taking special care to bin or burn any plants that appear diseased.
- Pick any remaining green tomatoes in the greenhouse and then compost the plants if they appear healthy.

CLEAR UP any dead or diseased leaves on vegetable plants. Even if the leaves are not parts of the plant you would normally eat, this is well worthwhile doing because you will remove potential sources of overwintering infections and problems for the following year.

After you have harvested the last of your climbing French or runner beans, cut back the top growth and compost it. By leaving the root system in the soil you will be getting a bit of free fertiliser, as the roots of peas and beans contain nitrogen-fixing bacteria which help to raise available nitrogen levels in the soil for crops the following year. By the time you get around to using the space next year the roots will have rotted away, so there will be nothing left to clear up and the nutrient levels will be improved.

Sow yourself a flowerpot full of basil seed and keep it either in a propagator or on a warm sunny window sill until the seedlings appear. This herb is very tender, so would not withstand temperatures outdoors at this time of year. However, it makes a great window sill potted herb and is terribly easy to raise in this way.

If you are fond of fresh mint or parsley, it is worth bringing indoors part of a clump of either of these herbs now. Just pot a chunk of the garden plant, complete with roots, into a reasonable-sized container of compost and keep it on a sunny or well-lit window sill, and you will be able to carry on enjoying their fresh flavours for the next few months.

Vegetables such as aubergines may still be continuing to fruit, but do harvest them as soon as you can, as sudden changes in temperatures are likely at this time of year and these will kill off the plants in their entirety, unless they are growing in a greenhouse. Light levels and temperatures are so much lower that the plants are unlikely to put on much new growth anyway, so it is best to harvest and cut your losses.

Tomatoes, peppers and aubergines that have finished cropping in greenhouses or porches should now be cleared away and composted. Do not risk composting anything that does not look completely healthy. Any unripened tomato fruits can still be persuaded to turn red if you place them in a good-sized paper bag, together with an overripe (freckled) banana. The ethylene gas given off by the banana will help to ripen the tomato fruits.

Sow and plant

- Now is your last chance to plant autumn onion sets and garlic (see page 126).

FRUIT

ESSENTIALS

If time is really short, try to fit these jobs in.

- Treat peach leaf curl with a copper-based fungicide.
- Tidy up strawberry plants.

IF PEACHES OR NECTARINES have been affected by peach leaf curl disease, apply a copper-based fungicide as the leaves fall. This will help to clean up the plant and reduce the risk of the problem next year. You will need to repeat the treatment at about two-week intervals in late January and February.

In a spare few minutes have a good tidy-up around any strawberry plants. Pick off old faded or diseased-looking leaves and cut off any remaining runners to ensure that the main plant keeps its vigour.

PONDS AND WATER FEATURES

ESSENTIALS

If time is really short, try to fit these jobs in.

- Reduce food given to pond fish.
- Regularly empty the net over the pond as it fills with leaves.
- Fit a net if you have not already done so.
- Pick or cut off deteriorating foliage from pond plants before it flops into the water.

IF YOUR POND includes fish, reduce the amount of food you give them as they now require considerably less than they did earlier on in the season. Excess food will decompose in the water and may result in toxic materials being formed.

Regularly remove the net over the surface of your pond and empty the leaves on to the compost heap. If you have not already got a net in place over the surface, fix one as a matter of urgency, but try to clear out any leaves from the water first (see page 128).

Continue to remove dead and dying foliage from pond and marginal plants regularly.

PROBLEM OF THE MONTH: FUNGI

Fungi of all types are likely to appear all over the place in the autumn and because there are rarely any significant frosts until late this month or even later, many will survive for several days or longer. Most toadstools that appear in gardens are not harmful to plants, so there is no need to panic as soon as you see them. If they appear on lawns, just brush them off to minimise their spread, unless they appear in circles or look as if they are killing off the grass. However, a few, such as the tough bracket fungi that develop on tree trunks and the golden toadstools of honey fungus, can spell trouble. Some fungi may cause a tree to become potentially dangerous and even if you remove the fungus itself, the problem may continue to develop. If in any doubt it is best to consult an expert.

November

Winter may be just around the corner but there is still plenty to enjoy in your garden. True, you may find you need to wear a layer or two more as temperatures plummet, but who cares when there is that wonderfully Novemberish feel to the air and when so many trees and shrubs are still decked with the last of their fiery display of reds, oranges and golds, some studded with brightly coloured berries?

Heavy dews and frosts are commonplace and the garden is definitely moving towards its slow-moving wintry state – and yes, you can slow down too; but make sure you allow yourself a little bit of time in the garden to enjoy what's there and get on with a bit of constructive healthy outdoor exercise.

GENERAL TASKS

MOST AREAS OF THE GARDEN will now be looking as if they have been hit by winter: those first few frosts will have caused foliage to flop and stems to sink downwards. Do some tidying, making sure that you clear up any pest- or diseases-ridden plants, but make sure that you don't go too far, as old stems and leaves can really help provide necessary winter protection for the more frost-susceptible plants, and at the same time offer much-needed shelter to insects and other small creatures.

Wild birds may appear to have a good supply of food in and around your garden at this time of year, but don't forget them completely – remember that the RSPB now advocate feeding throughout the year. Scrub down bird tables again and wash out feeders to minimise the risk of your feathered friends catching diseases.

Windy wintery weather can do a lot of damage to climbers, so it is essential that new growth is tied in properly before the worst of the weather arrives

TREES, SHRUBS AND CLIMBERS

ESSENTIALS

If time is really short, try to fit these jobs in.

- Insulate containers to decrease the risk of roots freezing.
- Prune deciduous hedging as necessary.
- Get planting, provided the soil is neither too wet nor frozen.

APPLY A BULKY ORGANIC MULCH around the base of trees, shrubs and climbers to help retain soil moisture during drier months and to keep weeds down.

Provide a little protection for recently planted trees, shrubs and climbers, as these may be unusually soft, even if they are plants that you regard (and which their label implies) are perfectly hardy. Sharp winds and frosts can do a lot of damage, but a couple of layers of fleece or a temporary windbreak should make a lot of difference and help avoid problems.

Insulate pots of trees or shrubs growing in containers (see page 15).

Protect favourite plants from rabbits if you have these pests in your garden. Pretty as they may look, there is no doubt that rabbits can cause a lot of damage, particularly once their favourite food supplies start to decline. Chicken mesh around individual plants works well; but if the problem is bad, the best solution is to fence off the whole garden with chicken mesh, including any gates. The holes in the mesh need to be small in diameter (about 2cm/ ³/₄ in) and the mesh at least 90–100cm (36–38in) tall, with an additional 15cm (6in) buried below ground and slanting outwards. Erecting this is a time-consuming job, and if you are fencing the whole garden it may be something you decide to get a professional to do; and the initial outlay may seem off-putting, but it is a small price to pay for winning a constant battle against plant-munching rabbits!

Sort out old or overgrown deciduous hedging now, pruning it back hard to encourage new growth for next year. Evergreen hedges should not be tackled now.

Make sure that this year's shoots on climbers are properly tied in or else they may get pulled away from the framework during autumn and winter gales. It is a lot easier to do a bit of tying in now than a major sorting out once the damage has been done.

Prune out any dead, diseased or damaged wood on shrubs but avoid doing anything more than is really necessary at this time of year. Trees containing dead wood or dead limbs can pose a real hazard, but should be dealt with by a well-recommended professional, especially if they are large.

Sow and plant

• Towards the end of this month start planting bare-root trees, shrubs or hedging, or get your order in now for plants to be delivered in early winter (see page 151).

• For much of this month conditions should be good for planting, so provided the soil is neither unusually wet or cold, get any new plants in the ground promptly to allow them to establish before the onset of winter (see page 26).

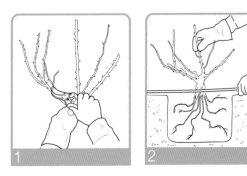

• Bare-root and container-grown roses can be planted now, and make great additions to any garden. Specialist rose nurseries offer a far greater range of bare-root roses than most garden centres. Climbing or rambling forms can transform a pergola or archway and if planted now establish particularly well. Ramblers have stems that are somewhat more flexible than climbers so are especially useful over arches and pergolas. When planting a bare-root rose, make sure that the roots are spread out really well in the planting hole. If necessary soak the roots for a couple of hours before planting and prune out anything that is much longer than the majority or diseased or damaged. Incorporate plenty of bulky organic matter into and around the planting hole. Place a cane over the top of the planting hole to help you gauge the correct planting depth: the slightly swollen area or graft point needs to be just at the soil level.

Planting bare-root roses

1 Prune out any dead, diseased or damaged stems on the bare root rose, pruning back to a healthy looking outward-facing bud.

2 Place a cane over the top of the planting hole to make it easier to gauge where the soil level will be. Spread the roots out well and position the rose so that the graft point is just on the soil surface.

FLOWERS

ESSENTIALS

If time is really short, try to fit these jobs in.

- Tidy up diseased leaves and remove fallen leaves from beds and borders.
- Heap a mulch over the crowns of tender herbaceous perennials and bulbs.
- Plant tulips and lilies.
- Plant herbaceous perennials.

Lilies add elegance, colour and often a truly delightful and inescapable perfume and can be planted now

TIDY UP flower beds and borders. Removing at least some of the dead stems and leaves will make the whole place look better; take a little more time over this job and you can make it much more useful. It is essential to remove diseased stems and leaves, but try to leave at least some of the top growth (see page 119). I always leave stout, sturdy stems such as those on sedums and grasses because they look beautiful when covered with a hoar frost.

Cut back the top growth on ornamental grasses that do not look attractive at this time of year. You can leave those that still look good until early spring.

Continue to rake up fallen leaves from flower beds and from the crowns of plants. A garden vacuum will make the job a lot easier and quicker, as well as reducing the risk of damage to the plants themselves.

Protect less hardy bulbs such as agapanthus and nerines by heaping some mulch over the area where they are planted.

Thin out the canes on established bamboos. The extra space the remaining canes will have will allow them to have more freedom to move as a clump of bamboo should. You can use the canes you have thinned out for plant supports next year, or for border edging.

Lift and divide congested or over-mature clumps of herbaceous perennials (see page 119). As soil conditions get colder and wetter, this job gets trickier and the plants tend to respond less well, so if in doubt, wait until the spring. In most areas however the weather should be fine for at least most of this month.

Sow and plant

- Plant tulips and lilies in beds and borders, and in containers (see page 122). Garden centres should have a good range available, especially if you shop early in the month.

- Herbaceous perennials should establish well if planted this month, as there is still enough warmth in the soil to get their roots growing. If the ground is very wet, however, delay until it dries out a bit.

- Send off for a good selection of seed catalogues if you are planning to sow seed in late winter or spring. Giving yourself plenty of time with the catalogues is a good investment because it will allow you to check out all the best varieties and those that show particular resistance to pests and diseases too.

THE LAWN

ESSENTIALS
If time is really short, try to fit these jobs in.

- Clear autumn leaves from the lawn regularly.
- When wet, avoid walking on the lawn.

CLEAR FALLEN LEAVES from the lawn surface, using a spring-tined rake, and add them to a leaf mould heap (see page 129). If a few fallen twigs are incorporated this does not matter.

If there has been a lot of rain, avoid walking on the lawn if possible.

Brush toadstools off the lawn surface, using a besom or broom.

PROBLEM OF THE MONTH: CORAL SPOT FUNGUS

Bright orange raised spots on woody stems are the fruiting bodies of coral spot fungus. During damp weather the spores of this fungus spread rapidly and can colonise dead or damaged wood. Once coral spot is in a stem on some plants it may show more aggressive tendencies and cause dieback. This is a common problem, seen especially frequently on acers, figs, magnolias and elaeagnus.

- Prune out infected stems as soon as you notice them, cutting right back to completely healthy wood. Bin or burn the prunings.
- Try to remove dead stems regularly even before the fungus appears.

HERBS AND VEGETABLES

ESSENTIALS

If time is really short, try to fit this job in.

- Insulate pots of herbs.

INSULATE POTS containing herbs to prevent the plant roots from becoming frozen. Check that drainage holes are not obstructed and place pots on 'feet' to keep drainage holes clear.

FRUIT

ESSENTIALS

If time is really short, try to fit this job in.

- Send off for catalogues from specialist fruit tree nurseries.

TOWARDS THE END OF THE MONTH you can start pruning apples and pears (see page 155). This is very much a winter pruning, so if you prefer you could leave it for a month or two.

Prune redcurrants, blackcurrants and gooseberries if you have not already done so (see pages 18 and 101).

Sow and plant

• As soon as fruit trees and bushes are dormant they can be planted in a bare-root state – in most areas this is from the end of November onwards. The widest range is usually available from specialist nurseries, so if you are considering planting fruit, get some catalogues so that you can order what you need promptly (see page 19).

PONDS AND WATER FEATURES

CUT BACK FADED AND DETERIORATING foliage from pond and marginal plants before it flops in to the water.

FIXTURES AND FITTINGS

CHECK ARCHES, arbours, trellis and fencing. These are likely to need repairing from time to time, and autumn winds often cause a bit of damage or loosening. The great thing about checking them now is that once the leaves have fallen from climbers it is much easier to see the structure or perhaps even carefully remove the plants before carrying out any necessary repair work, which you should get to work on as soon as possible.

If you are sure you will not use furniture over the winter then consider covering it up or moving it to a garage or shed. This will help to prolong its life, particularly if it is made of wood, and also reduce the amount of time you need to spend cleaning it up before it can be used next year.

Opposite: As foliage starts to deteriorate it may flop in to the water, so this needs to be cleared at the same time as you remove any leaves which have fallen in from nearby trees

December

There may not be much movement from the plants in your garden, but if you get the chance it is still worthwhile getting out there and doing some work. Provided you avoid any wet weather and can choose one of those beautiful, bright, yet crisp December days, this is a perfect month for doing some seriously hard physical work as you will find that your capacity is a lot greater than when you have the sun beating down on your shoulders. I often get the urge to have a bit of a sort-out at this time of year, perhaps making some harsh but necessary decisions about plants that have really passed their best and at the same time having a serious pre-spring tidy-up.

It may be OK to leave sorting out your house until spring arrives, but your garden will really appreciate some action now. Provided the soil is not too wet, it is also a great time to get on with digging in or incorporating manure. You will be amazed at how refreshing even a short burst of such activity in the garden can be, at a time of the year when you might have been spending far too much time being a couch potato!

GENERAL TASKS

CHECK THAT INSULATION on outside pipes is properly in place and, if you have not already done so, use several layers of bubble-wrap polythene to lag the pipework. If you make an easily removable 'hood'-shape for your outside tap you should be able to continue to use the tap during milder spells of weather, replacing the hood when you have finished. It may also be worth considering isolating an outside tap from the mains.

A garden can look beautiful in the depths of winter, but if you include a few bird feeders you will encourage wildlife to brighten it up further

Don't forget to ensure that garden birds have a plentiful supply of water and suitable food. Replenish water regularly so that it is fresh and not constantly frozen, and put up bird feeders, peanuts or seed dispensers, making use of any raised flat surfaces for feeding those birds that are less acrobatic. At this time of year food for birds can be in really short supply, which may result in fatalities, so do your bit for them now so that they will be there in your garden for you to look at later in the year. And don't forget that many birds are useful predators of many common garden pests.

If you need a brief spell of activity to warm you up, rake up fallen leaves from the lawn or the soil surface. Even if you thought you had done quite a good job in the autumn the chances are there will still be quite a lot that have accumulated or redistributed themselves. You can then collect up piles of leaves and use them to make leaf mould.

When tidying up around the garden, take the opportunity to have a pest and disease hunt as well. The number of active creatures that you see will be fairly small, but you may well find pests such as hibernating snails, which are easily rounded up now. It is also worth keeping a pair of secateurs and a bucket or other container to hand for dealing with any obviously infested or infected leaves or stems that you find. There is no doubt that a winter clean-up like this will help to keep problems down during the spring and summer months, but don't be too tidy: remember that many harmless and beneficial insects need places in which to hide and breed – and the odd fallen leaf or twig is often perfect.

Treat yourself to some time out in other people's gardens. Garden visiting maybe something you associate with the summer months, but believe me it can be even more fantastic on a cold, yet sunny winter's day. And what better way to gain inspiration about plants that you too could grow in your garden to bring colour, perfume and structure at a time of year that is all too often regarded as a bit bleak. It is worth checking the local newspaper and garden guides, including the 'Yellow Book' – the National Gardens Scheme's annual guide to gardens open for charity – for information on gardens in your area that are particularly attractive at this time of year. Don't forget to take your notebook with you.

TREES, SHRUBS AND CLIMBERS

ERECT A TEMPORARY WINDBREAK around evergreens that were planted in the autumn, particularly if you live in a windy or cold area. These are likely to be susceptible to wind scorching, because they are not yet well established and also have relatively tender foliage, and a windbreak will help to prevent such damage. This may seem like yet another job to do, but it is essential, especially for conifers, which once scorched are unlikely to produce much in the way of replacement growth and so the plants may be permanently damaged.

Prune deciduous shrubs and trees now if any fairly large-scale work is necessary. One of the great advantages of doing this during the winter is that there are no leaves on the plant and so there is less mess to clean up afterwards. You will also find that it is easier to work out what you need to do when you are faced with a framework of dormant, leafless branches rather than a foliage-clad mass. Always take out any dead, diseased, damaged or dying wood as priority. Make sure that you do not leave stubs of wood (which encourage dieback) and that you do not remove the branch collar if you are taking off sizeable limbs. Any really large-scale work should be carried out by a reputable tree surgeon or arborculturist.

If you are doing a lot of tree and shrub pruning, consider borrowing, hiring or even buying a chipper. Unless it is infected with diseases (such as canker), the pruned material is potentially very useful in the garden once chipped. Wood chip can be used as a mulching material or to make woodland-style path surfaces. It can also be mixed with fairly soft, high-nitrogen materials such as grass clippings during the summer months. If you have ever been faced with large quantities of cut grass and are not sure what to do with them, the chippings could be your best ally, as when you mix these together the high-nitrogen and moisture content of the grass helps to rot down the chippings, and the presence of the chippings helps to keep the structure of the grass clippings, and so prevent that nasty, evil-smelling, slimy mass which you may have experienced before.

A dusting of frost and a few spiders' webs add extra charm to the spiky foliage and red berries of a holly at this time of year

Provided it is not frosty, deciduous hedges can still be successfully pruned now

Check trees, shrubs and climbers planted in the autumn for loosening by any recent windy weather or heavy frosts. Do this regularly – it will only take a minute or two – and, if necessary, carefully re-firm their root balls into the soil. If left exposed to extreme winter weather the roots will be readily damaged and this could cause lasting problems.

Provided the soil is not frozen solid or excessively wet, it is still feasible to move any trees or shrubs that you now feel you have planted in the wrong position. There is always a degree or risk associated with doing this, but provided you do it carefully and while the plant is not in active growth, you are in with a chance (see page 118).

If you have a holly tree that is in berry, try to ensure that there will be a few berries left for you by the end of the month. It is lovely to have a few real holly berries in your house over Christmas, but birds in particular often feast on these fruits and so often come Christmas there are none to be had. Cover a stem or two loosely with netting or fleece to keep the birds off, but make sure you do this early in the month or else there will be nothing left to cover.

Reduce the length of the stems on any tall rose bushes to decrease the risk of their being moved in the ground by the wind. Doing this by about 50 per cent will greatly decrease the wind resistance. This is a quick and not necessarily accurate pruning job, taking only a few minutes. Come the spring you will need to prune the rose properly and neatly, but there is no need to worry about that right now.

Knock heavy snowfall off the branches of trees and shrubs. I love to see a carpet of snow on the garden and all the plants in it, but snowfall can sometimes spoil the shape of trees and shrubs, and if the snow thaws slightly and then re-freezes, it is more likely to cause damage, so this is a job worth doing. Conifers in particular may have their structure ruined by heavy snowfall, particularly if they are upright types their branches may be pulled outwards and downwards, so treat these as priority.

If you find keeping up with hedge trimming difficult, you can get on and trim deciduous hedges now, provided the weather is not really frosty (see page 141). Conifer hedges should definitely be left until the weather warms up.

Check that stakes and ties on any recently planted trees are still in good condition and in the correct position, so that they cannot damage the plant and yet are still doing the job they need to. This is particularly important if you live in a windy area.

Sow and plant

• Continue to plant trees, shrubs and climbers, provided the soil is neither frozen solid nor too wet. Bare-root plants are available now – including roses (see page 141) – and are often considerably less expensive than container-grown ones (see page 26).

• Creating a hedge from bare-root whips or 'rooted sticks' is easy and very inexpensive. These are available throughout the dormant period but for best results plant them this month or early next while there is no chance that they will start to move into growth – come February buds may start to break in milder seasons and warmer areas. Bare-root whips of native species make a great hedge, perfect for attracting wildlife in either a rural or a town garden. Dig the soil over, incorporating some well-rotted manure or compost if possible, and then plant the whips at about 45cm (18in) spacings. For a denser, more impenetrable hedge, plant two parallel, staggered rows. Water in if the soil is at all dry and protect against rabbits or deer if there is any chance that either of these could be a problem. Galvanised chicken wire works well against rabbits (see page 140), and helps against deer at least while the plants are still small. To save yourself a lot of time in the long term, consider planting the whips through landscape fabric. This is a woven synthetic material, which allows water to penetrate but goes a long way towards keeping weeds away, so preventing competition and saving you a huge amount of weeding time later on. Place it along the hedge line, anchor the sides and then make a gash through which to plant each whip. Once you have finished planting, just cover the fabric with wood chip to hide it.

Opposite: *Why not fill
containers now empty of
summer bedding to create
a fantastic autumn and
winter display of foliage
and flowers?*

FLOWERS

PROVIDE WINTER PROTECTION for any perennials that are not completely hardy if you did not do so earlier in the year (see page 120) and protect containers (see page 15). The coldest weather is usually still yet to come.

If you have not already done so, provide adequate winter protection for trees, shrubs or climbers that are not fully hardy. This is particularly important in colder regions or if the plants have not been in the ground for that long. Often protection is necessary in the first winter, but you may find that once the plant is better established you do not need to do this.

Leave any snow that falls on overwintering flowers in beds, borders or containers. It is unlikely to do any direct damage and indeed it often acts as an insulating blanket, protecting the plant against even harsher conditions and fluctuating temperatures.

Clear from alpine or rock garden plants any leaves that have fallen from nearby trees or shrubs. Many of these plants react particularly badly to moisture around their crowns, but taking a few moments to do this will ensure that air circulation remains good around them.

Cut back really deteriorated growth on herbaceous perennials. Ideally I like to keep some top growth for as much of the winter as possible. However, if the plant has started to look messy, or the leaves are becoming rotten and slimy, it is usually best to remove the growth and compost it. Take the opportunity to check for pests such as slugs and snails as you do this.

Sow and plant

• If your garden needs an instant facelift, don't forget that you can still plant up a container or two for winter interest. If you use a really large container such as a half barrel which decreases the chances of the compost and plant roots being damaged by cold, you could plant a small shrub or miniature tree in the centre (something like pieris or a clipped, variegated holly or box is perfect) and then plant around the base of this with winter-interest bedding plants, which you could change as the seasons progress. Such a container would thus make a feature in the garden that is permanently good-looking.

• Don't delay ordering a few packets of seed or even pop down to the local garden centre and buy a few off the shelf. Choose seeds now and the range is greater than it will be when it is time to get sowing. If you have not grown from seed before, consider growing hardy annual seeds – a way of producing a mass of colour inexpensively and with amazingly little effort (see page 38).

• If you visit your favourite garden centre, you may be tempted by an array of reduced-price spring-flowering bulbs. Ideally bulbs like this should be planted as promptly as possible and it is obviously essential to ensure that they are not 'fungusy' before you buy them, but I have had great success with a whole range of spring-flowering bulbs planted this month. If your soil is wet or extremely cold, remember that most bulbs, including tulips, daffodils and other narcissus, scillas and lilies, look fantastic in containers, so get planting.

PROBLEM OF THE MONTH: APPLE CANKER

Loose areas of bark develop, often in concentric rings, forming cankers, which are sometimes sunken or swollen. If the canker rings the branch, it causes dieback. In extreme cases whole limbs may be killed. In the summer tiny raised white fungal pustules develop on the cankered area and in winter tiny red raised fruiting bodies develop. The causal fungus *Nectria galligena* commonly attacks pears and apples but may also attack other trees such as willows, poplar and sorbus.

• Prune out infected areas completely, cutting back to healthy growth, and bin or burn the prunings.

THE LAWN

TRY YOUR VERY HARDEST to keep off the surface of your lawn if it is either very wet or covered in a layer of frost (see page 16).

Continue to clear leaves, using a spring-tined rake or even a besom, but avoid raking them up during damp weather unless you are able to do so from a nearby path (see above). Leaves on a lawn surface at this time of year are inclined to get soggy and may not be that easy to rake up, but if you leave them in place the grasses beneath soon start to die off and you can be left with a real mess come the spring.

Scatter worm casts on the lawn surface (see page 16).

During mild weather it may still be possible to repair damaged lawns by laying turf or turning it (see page 40). However, if in any doubt about the weather ahead, it is probably best to leave this job until the spring.

HERBS AND VEGETABLES

IF THE SOIL IS NOT WET, get on and dig over any areas in which you intend to plant or sow vegetables. Incorporating plenty of well-rotted manure or garden compost will help to improve the soil's texture as well as its fertility, and the frost that is likely to be on its way will help to break down heavy clay soils and make them slightly more manageable.

Pots of herbs growing in containers may need some frost protection, so wrap the sides of the pot with a couple of layers of bubble-wrap polythene or hessian. Where possible moving them closer to a warm and sheltered house wall will also help. Take care to leave all parts of the foliage uncovered and also leave the base of the pot clear for good drainage.

Sow and plant

• Take time to have a good peruse of a selection of seed catalogues and make sure that you get your order in promptly for any vegetable seeds, onion sets, garlic bulbs and seed potatoes you will need over the next few months.

• If you have a heated propagator and somewhere to keep plants until they are ready to be planted out, sow yourself a few pots or small trays of radishes or lettuce. Provided you have a sunny and relatively warm window sill about 13°C (55°F), an unheated propagator will do.

FRUIT

ESSENTIALS

If time is really short, try to fit these jobs in.

- Check stakes and ties.
- Continue to prune as necessary.

TAKE A FEW MOMENTS to check ties and stakes on any fruit trees to ensure that they are still keeping the tree in the correct position and have not become loosened or damaged (see page 17).

Continue to carry out winter pruning on apples and pears, always making sure that you prune out any dead, diseased or damaged branches as a priority. Apple canker is likely to be a particular problem. This may show up as flaky patches of bark, usually in concentric rings in an oval shape and associated with dieback. All cankered areas should be cut out promptly and the debris binned or burned. You can also prune trained fruit trees now (see page 18).

Prune currants if you have not already (see pages 18 and 101).

Sow and plant

- Provided the soil is neither excessively wet nor frozen solid, plant fruit bushes and fruit trees (see page 13).

PONDS AND WATER FEATURES

ESSENTIALS

If time is really short, try to fit these jobs in.

- Take precautions to prevent the surface of the pond from freezing over completely.
- Thaw a hole in the ice on the surface if a pond becomes frozen over.

PREVENT PONDS from icing over completely during cold weather to avoid a build-up of toxic gases and damage to fish or pond wildlife and cracking of liners (see page 19).

If the surface does become frozen, thaw a hole in the ice (see page 19).

FIXTURES AND FITTINGS

DURING DRY and relatively mild spells, treat any wooden structures in the garden with a suitable wood treatment (see page 20).

Clean algae and mosses from smooth, hard surfaces to prevent them from becoming slippery and dangerous. Try to work out if there is anything causing the surface to be regularly wetted – perhaps paving slabs need re-levelling so that dips are not being created, or perhaps guttering needs to be cleared to prevent excessive quantities of water falling on to a relatively small area. Use a power washer if you have one – this will certainly save you a lot of time – or by using a yard broom or stiff scrubbing brush, possibly combined with a proprietary patio cleaner to scrub the algae and moss off the areas.

If you have a cold frame or a greenhouse that is relatively empty of plants at this time of year, choose a relatively mild day when it has been dry for a while and take the opportunity to clean up and if necessary treat any wooden surfaces. It is much easier to do this sort of job when there are relatively few plants to move about. It is essential to take any plants out of the way, as chemical drips or in some cases even fumes can do a lot of damage.

Construct

- Make a pergola, arch or arbour, or build one from a kit (see page 20).

A stiff brush and soapy water is usually all that is needed to clear algae and other deposits from hard surfaces

ACKNOWLEDGEMENTS

Thanks to Celia Kent who has been by my side throughout, Heather Holden-Brown (now sadly both ex-Headline, but great to work with), Anne Askwith for her editing skills, Mel Watson for some fabulous picture research and Sarah Heneghan for the special photography.

INDEX

Page references in *italics* refer to illustrations